50 WINNING DUPLICATE T[...]
for the improving tournament pla[...]

Many competent players are frustrated by an apparent inability to score well at duplicate pairs. No matter how hard they try, the secret of success seems to lie forever beyond reach. The truth is that playing good bridge is not enough to win at pairs. The regular winners are those who have learned to adapt their strategy to take account of the vagaries of match-point scoring. A small shift in emphasis can make a big difference to results.

In this book Australian expert Ron Klinger shows you how to do it. There are five sections covering constructive bidding, competitive bidding, opening leads, declarer play and defence, and they are full of well-chosen example hands and sound advice. Put these tips into practice and your results are sure to improve.

Ron Klinger scored a great success with *100 Winning Bridge Tips* which is now in its fifth impression. *50 Winning Duplicate Tips* has proved itself equally popular.

'This book is strongly recommended for those who wish to improve their results at duplicate pairs.' – Hugh Kelsey, *The Scotsman*

by RON KLINGER *in the Master Bridge Series*

*GUIDE TO BETTER CARD PLAY
GUIDE TO BETTER ACOL BRIDGE
100 WINNING BRIDGE TIPS
50 WINNING DUPLICATE TIPS
PLAYING TO WIN AT BRIDGE
THE MODERN LOSING TRICK COUNT
FIVE-CARD MAJORS
BRIDGE WITHOUT ERROR
IMPROVE YOUR BRIDGE MEMORY
WORLD CHAMPIONSHIP PAIRS BRIDGE
BASIC BRIDGE: A Guide to Good Acol Bidding and Play
ACOL BRIDGE MADE EASY
TEACH YOUR CHILD BRIDGE
ACOL BRIDGE FLIPPER
BASIC ACOL BRIDGE FLIPPER
DUPLICATE BRIDGE FLIPPER
FIVE-CARD MAJORS BIDDING FLIPPER
MODERN LOSING TRICK COUNT FLIPPER
STANDARD BRIDGE FLIPPER
MASTER OPENING LEADS
MASTER PLAY AT TRICK 1
MASTER CUE BIDDING TO SLAMS
MASTER DOUBLES

with David Bird
KOSHER BRIDGE

with Hugh Kelsey
INSTANT GUIDE TO STANDARD BRIDGE

* Winner of the 1991 *Book of the Year Award* of the American Bridge
Teachers' Association

50 WINNING DUPLICATE TIPS
for the improving tournament player

RON KLINGER

LONDON
VICTOR GOLLANCZ LTD
in association with
PETER CRAWLEY
1992

TO KEITH
who epitomises friendship

First published in Great Britain 1991
in association with Peter Crawley
by Victor Gollancz Ltd,
14 Henrietta Street, London WC2E 8QJ
Second impression January 1992

The right of Ron Klinger to be identified as
author of this work has been asserted by him in
accordance with the Copyright, Designs and
Patents Act 1988

British Library Cataloguing in Publication Data
Klinger, Ron
    50 winning duplicate tips. —(Master bridge series)
    1. Duplicate bridge
    I. Title II. Series
    795.415

ISBN 0-575-05052-7

Photoset in Great Britain by
Rowland Phototypesetting Ltd,
Bury St Edmunds, Suffolk
and printed by St Edmundsbury Press Ltd,
Bury St Edmunds, Suffolk

CONTENTS

Introduction

100 Winning Bridge Tips (Gollancz/Peter Crawley, 1987) was written for
the improving player to boost the general level of bridge, whether it was
rubber bridge, teams play or matchpoint pairs. This book is written for
the pairs players since most tournament players find themselves playing
matchpointed pairs either exclusively or most of the time. Teams play is
popular at the higher levels, but at the average club there would be at
least twenty pairs sessions for every session of teams.

50 Winning Duplicate Tips is designed for the improving tournament
player. Pairs play is quite different from rubber bridge and the secret of
winning at pairs is bound up with the scoring method. At rubber you are
rewarded by the score you obtain. The size of the score is relevant. At
pairs, the size of the score is generally irrelevant. The sole question is:
How many pairs did your score beat? Not by how much did you beat
them, but simply did you beat their score? You are given points for each
pair that you beat on each board, whether you beat them narrowly or
whether you outscore them by a lot. The yardstick for success is thus not
size of the score but the frequency of outscoring your opponents. Your
real opponents at pairs are not the players against whom you play each
deal but the other pairs who are sitting in the same direction as you and
against whose results your scores will be compared.

The *Tips* are aimed at providing the best strategy for your bidding, play
and defence at matchpointed pairs. The expert pairs player will be
familiar with the ideas in these tips. Equally, the expert will not be eager
to share that knowledge with you. He prefers to maintain his edge as long
as possible.

If you can apply even 50% of the advice in these *Tips*, you will narrow the
gap between yourself and the expert. You will find your scores improving
and you will be winning more sessions and tournaments. There is
nothing that matches the euphoria of winning. And, who knows?
Perhaps it will not be long before you find yourself finishing in front of
your club's accepted top players. Perhaps they will be coming to you to
ask how you found the winning move. If so, do not lend them a copy of
this book. Make them go out and buy their own.

Ron Klinger
1991

PART 1: CONSTRUCTIVE BIDDING

The nature of duplicate requires an understanding of the scoring. You are not rewarded for the score you achieve. You gain only if your score is better than the scores of other pairs, no matter by how little.

This leads to the strategy of duplicate bidding. Safety is not your primary concern, but rather the frequency of gain. How often will your action work? If success exceeds 50%, it is a sound strategy, even though the size of the loss may be horrendous when a loss does occur.

Basic strategy at pairs is to avoid 5 ♣ or 5 ◇ at all costs if 3NT is at all feasible. Choose 4 ♡ or 4 ♠ with 8 or more trumps rather than 3NT. Not only is the major suit game safer, it will usually outscore 3NT. Prefer 3NT, however, when you have no better than a 7-card major fit unless the bidding reveals that 3NT is unsound.

The following tips for opening and responding will supplement your basic strategy.

TIP 1

In third seat after two passes, be prepared to open any hand which would be a sound overcall, even as low as 8–9 HCP.

If partner can rely on your opening in third seat only with a decent suit, partner will be quick to lead that suit if the bidding reveals your opening was underweight. This will be so even if your opening was 1 ♣ or 1 ◇, suits that do not normally have great lead-directing significance.

Ask yourself 'If right-hand opponent would have opened 1 ♣, would I have wanted to overcall?' If the answer is yes, you should open in third seat.

Even a strong 4-card major is acceptable for those playing 5-card majors. An excellent guide is the Suit Quality Test which can be found in detail in *100 Winning Bridge Tips* (Tip 26):

A suit is strong enough for an overcall if:
    Length in suit + Honours in that suit = Tricks to be bid.
    (The jack and ten are counted only if higher honours are also held.)

For the superlight third seat opening, the suit quality should be 8. If the suit quality is 7, the suit should contain at least two of the top three honours.

These hands are all suitable for third seat openings:

(A) ♠ A K J 8 5	(B) ♠ 8 7	(C) ♠ 8 7	(D) ♠ 9 7 3 2
♡ 6 5	♡ 9 6	♡ A K Q 5	♡ Q 8
◇ 9 8 3	◇ K Q J 9 3	◇ 6 5 3 2	◇ 9 3 2
♣ 7 4 2	♣ Q 9 6 2	♣ 9 6 5	♣ K Q J 8

If playing weak twos, Hand A is suitable for a weak 2 ♠, particularly if not vulnerable.

Example:

Dealer North:

Nil vulnerable

WEST	NORTH	EAST	SOUTH
	No	No	1♣
1♡	1♠ ..		

```
                    ♠ K 9 8 3
                    ♡ 9
                    ◇ Q 10 7 4
                    ♣ Q 6 3 2
   ♠ 10 7 4                          ♠ A J 6
   ♡ A K J 8 7 2        N            ♡ Q 6 5 3
   ◇ K J             W     E         ◇ A 8 3
   ♣ 10 8               S            ♣ 9 5 4
                    ♠ Q 5 2
                    ♡ 10 4
                    ◇ 9 6 5 2
                    ♣ A K J 7
```

East-West are likely to buy the hand in some number of hearts. After the above start, North should lead a club. South will take two clubs and given careful defence, North-South should collect two more tricks. Holding East-West to 140 should be a fine result.

Without South's opening, North might hit on a spade lead which costs a trick after declarer ducks in dummy. A diamond lead gives declarer a club discard. In either case West will make 10 tricks.

If you do make a superlight opening, you must pass partner's reply. If you make a second bid (unless forced by partner), you confirm an opening bid with normal opening values. This means you may have to forego a superlight opening if there is a response which you are not prepared to pass. For example:

♠ A K J 6 2	After two passes, it is tempting to open 1 ♠. Certainly
♡ ---	your suit is good enough and you want a spade lead above
◇ 6 5 3 2	all. Still, you cannot afford 1 ♠, as you cannot handle a
♣ 8 7 4 3	2♡ response. Best is to open a weak 2 ♠, otherwise Pass.

Another example:

Dealer West:
Both vulnerable

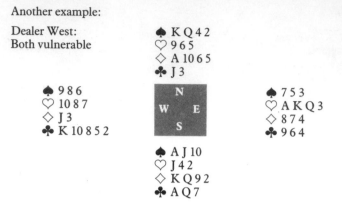

```
                    ♠ K Q 4 2
                    ♡ 9 6 5
                    ◇ A 10 6 5
                    ♣ J 3

  ♠ 9 8 6          N              ♠ 7 5 3
  ♡ 10 8 7      W     E           ♡ A K Q 3
  ◇ J 3            S              ◇ 8 7 4
  ♣ K 10 8 5 2                    ♣ 9 6 4

                    ♠ A J 10
                    ♡ J 4 2
                    ◇ K Q 9 2
                    ♣ A Q 7
```

After two passes, East should open 1 ♡. If East passes, North-South are likely to bid to 3NT. This is unbeatable on any lead, but if West decides to lead a club, this gives South 10 tricks and a bottom for East-West. After the 1 ♡ opening, West should prefer a heart lead and holding 3NT to nine tricks will give East-West well above average.

Even better, North-South may not be able to reach 3NT at all after the 1 ♡ opening. Neither has a heart stopper and no one can guarantee that East does not have five or six hearts. If North-South fail to reach game or try 4 ♠ or 5 ◇, East-West will score a near top, particularly on a heart lead.

TIP 2

If your choice is to remain in 1NT or support a minor at the 2-level, support the minor if your combined point count is under 22, but stay with 1NT if the combined count is 23-24.

The bidding starts 1 $\diamondsuit$: 1 $\heartsuit$, 1NT or similar. You have 4-card diamond support. Bid 2 $\diamondsuit$ if the point count total is up to 22, pass 1NT if you have 23-24. Even 22 is passable if your hand contains some 10s and 9s.

Where your side has only 20-21 points, 1NT is not safe and an overtrick is most unlikely. The minor suit partscore is more likely to produce a plus score. Revert to the minor.

Where your side has 23-24 points, 1NT is safe and an overtrick is quite likely. The minor suit contract will probably produce 9 tricks for +110 (10 tricks for +130 is not likely below 25-26 points) but 1NT with an overtrick gives you 120 and a better board.

For example:

Dealer North:
Both vulnerable

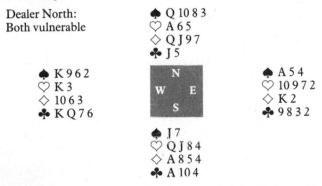

♠ Q 10 8 3
♡ A 6 5
♢ Q J 9 7
♣ J 5

♠ K 9 6 2
♡ K 3
♢ 10 6 3
♣ K Q 7 6

♠ A 5 4
♡ 10 9 7 2
♢ K 2
♣ 9 8 3 2

♠ J 7
♡ Q J 8 4
♢ A 8 5 4
♣ A 10 4

Playing a strong no-trump, South opened 1 $\diamondsuit$ in third seat. North responded 1 ♠ and South rebid 1NT. Holding 10 points, North left it in 1NT rather than support to 2 $\diamondsuit$.

West led a low club and South won with the 10. South continued with the $\heartsuit$ Q, covered by the king and taken by the ace. The $\diamondsuit$ Q came next, again covered and South won. South next led the $\diamondsuit$ 8 and let it run. When this worked, South had 2 hearts, 4 diamonds and 2 clubs, +120.

In a diamond partial, South is likely to lose 2 spades, 1 heart and 1 club, +110.

Dealer South:
Both vulnerable

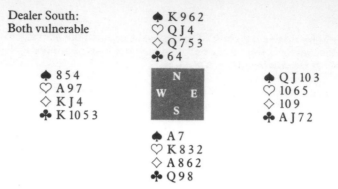

```
                    ♠ K 9 6 2
                    ♡ Q J 4
                    ◇ Q 7 5 3
                    ♣ 6 4
  ♠ 8 5 4                          ♠ Q J 10 3
  ♡ A 9 7          N               ♡ 10 6 5
  ◇ K J 4      W        E          ◇ 10 9
  ♣ K 10 5 3       S               ♣ A J 7 2
                    ♠ A 7
                    ♡ K 8 3 2
                    ◇ A 8 6 2
                    ♣ Q 9 8
```

Using a 15-17 1NT, South opened 1 ◇, North responded 1 ♠ and South rebid 1NT. With 8 points only, North reverted to 2 ◇ which was passed out. West led a club to the ace and East switched to the queen of spades. Declarer had no trouble ruffing a club and holding the losers to 1 heart, 1 diamond and 2 clubs for +110.

Had North passed 1NT, West would be likely to lead the club and the defence would take the first four tricks. The spade switch by West would also be marked and declarer would fail. Having to dislodge the ♡ A and ◇ K, declarer would lose the lead twice, allowing the defence to come to a spade trick before declarer can manage 7 tricks. Even if declarer made 1NT, +90 would rate poorly compared to the 110 available in 2 ◇.

Again, note that with 20-21-22 points, 1NT is not necessarily safe even when the opponents have no long suit to run. The minor suit partial is safer and when 1NT does make, the minor partial may still score better. With 23-24 points, however, 1NT is safer and an overtrick now is a reasonable chance, allowing +120.

TIP 3

After a 1♣ opening, if you have 4 diamonds and a 4-card major, prefer to respond 1♦ if in the 6-9 point range or with 16 or more points. In the 10-15 point range, bid the major as long as you have a comfortable no-trump rebid.

Partner has opened 1♣. What is your response with:

(A) ♠ 9 6 3	(B) ♠ K 6	(C) ♠ A J	(D) ♠ A J
♡ K Q 6 4	♡ A 9 6 3	♡ A 9 6 3	♡ A Q 6 3
◇ Q 7 5 3	◇ K J 7 5	◇ K J 7 5	◇ K Q J 5
♣ 7 5	♣ 7 5 2	♣ 7 5 2	♣ 7 5 2

Solutions: (A)   Respond 1◇. You have only 7 points and if partner has a minimum opening, you may be better off in a diamond partscore than in no-trumps (*see* Tip 2). For example:

WEST	EAST	WEST	EAST
♠ 5 4	♠ 9 6 3	1♣	1◇
♡ 8 3	♡ K Q 6 4	2◇	No
◇ A K 6 2	◇ Q 7 5 3		
♣ A J 8 6 2	♣ 7 5		

East-West have reached a sensible partscore and if North-South do compete in spades, East-West are well-placed to push on to 3◇. By contrast, what will happen if East responds 1♡? West will rebid 2♣ and play it there. East is not worth a second bid at the 2-level, certainly not a forcing change of suit. 2◇ should make 8 tricks and may make 9. 2♣ will be struggling to make 8. Even worse is a 1NT contract which is likely to go one off and maybe more.

Another reason to respond 1◇ with a very weak hand is that if there is a fit in hearts, opener has a chance to bid the hearts first. That will make the stronger hand the declarer, often an advantage when there is a significant disparity in the strengths of the hands.

One reason players have responded 1♡ in the past is the fear of an opponent intervening in spades. With the use of competitive doubles, this is no longer a threat (*see* Tip 11). If the bidding starts 1♣ : (No) : 1◇ : (1♠), opener can double for takeout to show a 4-card heart suit.

(B)   Respond 1♡. Here you have enough points to be comfortable in no-trumps. If opener rebids 1♠ or 2♣, you can continue with 2NT, inviting game. If opener is minimum and passes, you have sufficient to make it likely that 2NT will succeed and outscore a diamond partscore (*see* Tip 2).

As you have no intention or desire to play in diamonds with this strength, it will not harm you to mask your diamond holding. It may even be of benefit in no-trumps where you might welcome a diamond lead.

An immediate response in no-trumps is not recommended. If there is a fit in hearts, you are just as likely to make nine tricks in hearts (+140) as eight in no-trumps (120) opposite a minimum opening. There is no urgency to grab the no-trumps contract, despite your K-x in spades. There are many spade holdings with partner which make a no-trump contract from partner's side more appealing (for example, Q-10-x or A-J-x).

(C)   Respond 1 ♡. Again your plan is to play in hearts if partner has support or to rebid 3NT if nothing more exciting is revealed by partner's rebid. When slam is unlikely, avoid minor suit games. Concentrate on major suit fits and 3NT if no major fit is possible. As in (B), concealing your diamond holding may be beneficial in a no-trump game.

You wish to play in diamonds only if a slam is feasible. For that to be so, opener would need to be strong enough to reverse with 1 ♣ : 1 ♡, 2 ♢. Time enough then to indicate support for the diamonds.

(D)   Respond 1 ♢. Here you are strong enough for a slam in diamonds even opposite a minimum opening. If you respond 1 ♡, there is no convenient way later to bring the diamonds into play without distorting the shape of your hand.

WEST	EAST
♠ 5 4	♠ A J
♡ K 7	♡ A Q 6 3
♢ A 9 6 2	♢ K Q J 5
♣ K Q J 8 4	♣ 7 5 2

6 ♢ requires little more than a 3-2 diamond break and might survive a 4-1 break. It should be no problem after starting with 1 ♣ : 1 ♢, 2 ♢ . . .

If no fit comes to light and West reveals a minimum opening, East can always back into 3NT.

TIP 4

Where you have a major suit fit and also a hand reasonably suitable for no-trumps, play in the major if your combined point count is 25-29 but play in 3NT if the combined count is 30-31.

There are two reasons for preferring the major suit contract in general. 4 ♡ or 4 ♠ is usually safer than 3NT and when both contracts succeed, the major suit contract will usually outscore 3NT. All things being equal, you generally make one trick more in a decent suit fit than in no-trumps.

25-29 points: When you have just enough points for game, around the 25-29 mark, it is common enough for one suit to be unguarded. In that case, the trump suit protects you against the risk of the opponents running that long suit against you.

Even when you have every suit stopped, there is often one suit which has only one stopper, perhaps even two suits which are singly stopped. Once that stopper has been knocked out, you are at the mercy of their long suit when they regain the lead. Again, the trump contract protects you against their long suit. The real danger in no-trumps is not so much unguarded suits as short suits. It can be much safer to play 3NT with a suit of x-x-x opposite x-x-x than a suit of A-x opposite x-x.

For example:

Both vulnerable

WEST	EAST
♠ A 7 6 4 2	♠ K 9 5
♡ K Q 8 7	♡ A 6 3 2
◇ A 7	◇ K Q J
♣ 7 5	♣ 9 8 4

East-West should land in 4 ♡ (*see* Tip 5). Even 4 ♠ is superior to 3NT which might fail on a club lead. If you escape the club lead in 4 ♠ or 4 ♡, you might make 11 tricks if the majors behave as expected. Even if 3NT makes (clubs are 4-4 or a club is not led), you will do better most of the time in a major. Even on a club lead, you make 10 tricks (620 rather than 600) if the majors do not break badly.

With minimum game points, 25-29, when 3NT makes an overtrick for 430 or 630, you often find that the major suit game also scores the overtrick for 450 or 650.

WEST	EAST
♠ A 8 6	♠ Q J 10
♡ K Q 9 5	♡ A J 7 2
◇ A 7 4	◇ 9 6 3 2
♣ 9 6 2	♣ A Q

East-West should reach 4♡. If 3NT is reached and both black kings are onside, you will make 10 tricks. However, played in hearts with both black kings onside, barring the most fiendish breaks, you will make 11 tricks and outscore 3NT.

30-31 points: Now things tend to be different. You have so much strength, just short of a slam, that most suits are doubly stopped. An unguarded suit is possible but is a great rarity. A danger suit with just one stopper is possible but infrequent.

Here it is likely that you make 11 tricks whether it is no-trumps or trumps. You do not have quite enough for the slam and there are two losers regardless of the contract. Accordingly, it makes sense to play this strength hand in 3NT rather than 4-Major unless you have significant ruffing values.

WEST	EAST	
♠ K Q 9 7 3	♠ A J 4	4♠ is safe but 3NT is the spot at pairs. If the club finesse is on there are 12 tricks in either contract. Generally 3NT will outscore the spade game.
♡ K 5	♡ A 10 8	
◇ K Q 3	◇ A 9 8	
♣ 8 6 3	♣ K J 10 4	

WEST	EAST	
♠ J 8 2	♠ K Q	Although there is a fit in hearts, you will usually lose two tricks in hearts or in no-trumps even though 3NT could prove awkward. Take away the jack of
♡ K 10 6 4	♡ A Q 9 3	
◇ K Q 7	◇ J 8 6	
♣ A K 4	♣ Q 7 3 2	

spades and 4♡ is superior, but you cannot afford to worry about the odd case here and there.

WEST	EAST	
♠ A 8 6 4 2	♠ J 7 3	Here 3NT is vastly superior and 4♠ may fail on many layouts. If the ♡Q is onside and 4♠ comes home, those in 3NT also make 10 tricks. If the ♡Q is offside, 3NT will make but 4♠ may fail, not to
♡ 7 5	♡ K J 10	
◇ A 9 5	◇ K Q J	
♣ K J 4	♣ A Q 7 2	

mention the possibility of a 4-1 spade break. One of the great traps on hands in the 30-31 point zone is the weak trump suit.

TIP 5

Do not commit a hand to a 5-3 fit or a 5-4 major fit if a 4-4 major fit is feasible.

Playing 5-card majors, your partner opens 1 ♠. What action should you take with:

♠ A Q 3   ♡ K J 7 4   ◇ Q J 3 2   ♣ 7 6

Many players would commit the hand at once to a spade contract, via a forcing raise or a conventional strong supporting response (e.g. Swiss). This approach is not the best at pairs. Although perhaps not as safe, a 4-4 fit will normally generate at least the same number of tricks and often an extra trick, compared with a 5-3 fit or a 5-4 fit (or a 6-4 fit).

Suppose the two hands are:

WEST	EAST
♠ K J 8 7 6	♠ A Q 3
♡ A Q 5 2	♡ K J 7 4
◇ 7 4	◇ Q J 3 2
♣ A 5	♣ 7 6

Played in spades (or no-trumps) there are 10 tricks available, assuming the opponents attack clubs early enough. Played in hearts, there are 11 tricks if the hearts divide 3-2 (a 68% chance). After three rounds of hearts, declarer runs the spades and discards a club and a diamond. Result: No club loser. If hearts are trumps, a normal break allows you to score 5 heart tricks (4 in top cards and 1 by a ruff). If hearts are not trumps, you can obviously win only 4 tricks in the heart suit.

If hearts divide 4-1, you make only 10 tricks in 4♡ and score the same as those in spades. You cannot afford to leave any trumps out when you run the spades and therefore cannot score the club ruff. If hearts are 5-0, you will almost certainly fail in 4♡ on competent defence. The results are:

4♡ will outscore 4♠ whenever hearts are 3-2: 68% of the time
4♡ and 4♠ score the same when hearts are 4-1: 28% of the time
4♡ will do worse than 4♠ when hearts are 5-0: 4% of the time

Thus you do better in hearts 68% of the time and worse only 4% of the time. Even though 4♠ is safer, you cannot buck these odds at pairs.

The practical advice for East is to delay the support for the spades and respond 2◇. Here West bids 2♡ and East will raise the hearts. If West fails to show a heart suit, time enough then for East to support the spades.

A similar theme runs through these hands:

(1)   You open 1NT (12-14) and partner transfers to show 4 spades and 5 hearts. You hold:

♠ A 8 6 2
♡ A 7 6 3
♢ A 9 6
♣ J 6

Which suit should you support? Hearts figures to be the safer spot but the 4-4 spade fit is the place to be for the likely best score. Support the spades.

(2)   You open 1♣ Precision (16+ points) and partner responds 1♠, showing at least 5 spades and 8+ points. What action do you take with:

♠ K Q 5 2
♡ A Q 7 3
♢ A 8
♣ A 4 3

Do not raise the spades yet. Rebid 1NT (forcing since the 1♠ response created a game force) and await further information. Perhaps the hands are like this:

WEST	EAST
♠ K Q 5 2	♠ A J 7 6 3
♡ A Q 7 3	♡ K J 4 2
♢ A 8	♢ 7 5
♣ A 4 3	♣ 6 5

Raising spades is premature and would prevent the heart fit coming to light. In spades (or no-trumps), the limit is 11 tricks. In hearts, there are 12 tricks if the hearts divide 3-2. 6♡ is a sound contract while 6♠ is ridiculous.

(3)   You open 1♣ Precision and partner again responds 1♠. What is your rebid with:

♠ K Q 5 2
♡ A 2
♢ A J 5
♣ K 10 4 2

Again it could work out badly to raise the spades at once. There could be a superior contract. Suppose the hands are:

WEST	EAST
♠ K Q 5 2	♠ A 8 7 6 4 3
♡ A 2	♡ 8 4
♢ A J 5	♢ 6
♣ K 10 4 2	♣ A Q J 7

If West supports spades, East-West are unlikely to find their club fit and then the best East-West can do is reach 6NT or 6 ♠. In each case, the maximum potential is 12 tricks. If West marks time with 1NT, the club fit can be found and a grand slam in clubs would be a fitting reward.

Most players do not appreciate that a 4-4 fit can be superior to a 6-4 fit. Here, moreover, the 4-4 minor fit outscores the 6-4 major fit.

The tip is F.F.F.F.: Ferret For Four-Four Fit.

TIP 6

With a hand pattern of 4-3-3-3 opposite a 1NT opening, stay with
no-trumps and do not use Stayman if the 4-card suit is a major. With a
4-3-3-3 pattern opposite a possible 5-3-3-2, do not give support for
partner's 5-card major. If you have a stopper in each suit, a 5-3-3-2
opposite a 4-3-3-3 will produce the same number of tricks in no-trumps
as in the suit fit most of the time.

Consider these hands:

WEST	EAST
♠ A Q 6 5	♠ K J 7 4
♡ 8 3 2	♡ A Q 6
◇ K J 6	◇ A 5 4
♣ A 8 4	♣ 7 6 2

West opens 1NT (12-14) and East should raise to 3NT. If East tries
Stayman and finds the spade fit, 4 ♠ is clearly inferior to 3NT. If both
the ♡ K and ◇ Q are onside, both contracts make 10 tricks: 3NT scores
more. If one finesse works and the other fails, each contract makes 9
tricks: 3NT scores more. If both finesses fail, each contract makes 8
tricks: you still do better being in 3NT only one down.

Even if West's pattern is 4-4-3-2, 3NT may do as well:

WEST	EAST
♠ A Q 6 5	♠ K J 7 4
♡ K 3	♡ A Q 6
◇ K Q 6	◇ A 5 4
♣ 9 8 4 3	♣ 7 6 2

Here both contracts reckon to make 10 tricks almost all the time. The
chance of 5 or 6 cashing clubs on lead against 3NT is offset by the chance
of 4 rounds of clubs promoting a trump trick for the defence when spades
are 4-1.

The problem in these cases is the strength in the doubleton and whether a
ruff in that suit will provide an extra trick. The 4-4-3-2 opposite a 4-3-3-3
will produce an extra trick for the major 4-4 fit often enough. Here
modern relay systems have an advantage. They can determine opener's
exact pattern and play in 3NT when there is a 4-3-3-3 opposite a 4-3-3-3.
When the 4-3-3-3 faces a 4-4-3-2 and there is no exceptional strength
facing the doubleton, they can choose the 4-4 major fit. The more
strength there is opposite the doubleton, the more attractive 3NT
becomes.

When partner shows a 5-card major be reluctant to give 3-card support if your hand pattern is 4-3-3-3. With a weak hand, prefer 1NT. With a better hand, 2NT and 3NT may be available. The 3NT response should be restricted to a 4-3-3-3 pattern so that opener can safely remove to 4-Major if that appears prudent.

If partner is reluctant to accept no-trumps, you can then reveal the 3-card support. If partner accepts the no-trumps, this is likely to be your best spot.

For example:

WEST	EAST
♠ K Q 8 7 3	♠ J 6 5
♡ A 8 7	♡ K 6 5
♢ A 5	♢ K Q 7
♣ 8 7 4	♣ A 10 5 2

West would open 1 ♠ and East might reply 2 ♣ or 3NT. The partnership will do well to play in 3NT. On normal breaks, there will be 10 tricks whether the contract is no-trumps or spades. The absence of any ruffing value in the East hand means there is no benefit in choosing the trump contract. This is back to basics on how tricks are won: to play in a trump contract, you want to be able to ruff something. No ruffs, no-trumps; no shortage, no-trumps.

WEST	EAST	WEST	EAST
♠ A Q 9 8 5	♠ K 7 6 3	1 ♠	2 ♣
♡ A Q	♡ 9 7 5	2NT	3NT
♢ A 8 6	♢ K 7 2	No	
♣ Q 6 2	♣ A J 5		

West expects to take exactly the same number of tricks in spades as in no-trumps. If the heart finesse works, there are 11 tricks. If it loses, there are 10 tricks, assuming there is a club loser. If North leads a club away from the king, West scores an extra trick in each case.

Even if West's hearts were A-x, 3NT will do as well at least half the time. On a heart lead, if the club finesse is on, both contracts make 10 tricks. Without a heart lead, there are 10 tricks even if South has the king of clubs.

This last example is noteworthy since East has 4-card support and there is a 5-4 trump fit. Nevertheless, the 4-3-3-3 pattern opposite the 5-3-3-2 will not produce any extra tricks in the trump contract most of the time. And what works to produce the best score *most of the time* is the yardstick for pairs strategy.

TIP 7

When you have a 6-2 or 6-3 fit in a major, play in the major suit game rather than 3NT unless the suit is running and your outside winners do not need developing.

Suppose partner opens a weak 2♡. You hold:

(A)	♠ A 7 6	(B)	♠ A 7 6	(C)	♠ A K 6	(D)	♠ A 6 4
	♡ Q J 5		♡ Q J 5		♡ Q J 5 4		♡ Q J 5
	◇ A 9 4 2		◇ A 9 4 2		◇ A 9 4		◇ A 9 4 2
	♣ A 7 6		♣ K Q J		♣ A 7 6		♣ A Q J

In each case you use a 2NT enquiry and partner rebids 3◇, showing 6-8 points including two top honours in hearts. What action should you take in each case?

You quickly deduce that partner holds A-K-x-x-x-x in hearts and precious little else of value. It is now a matter of counting your tricks.

Hand A produces 9 tricks only, so you must avoid 4♡. However, the same 9 tricks are available in no-trumps. Rebid 3NT.

Hand B has 10 tricks but no-trumps is not safe. The opponents may lead spades or diamonds and establish tricks there. You have to lose the lead to knock out the ♣A and they may then cash too many tricks for your liking. Even if you just make 3NT, it will be a poor score with 4♡ also making. If you have to lose the lead to establish tricks, choose the trump contract.

Hand C has 10 winners in a heart contract but again they are instant winners. The same winners will perform in no-trumps. Despite your 10-card heart fit, you should play in 3NT.

Hand D has also 10 winners but the club finesse means you may have to lose the lead later. 3NT will score 11 tricks at least 50% of the time and 10 tricks some of the time. It is quite a reasonable gamble at pairs, particularly if you are looking for top scores to finish off a session or an event.

Suppose partner opens a weak 2♡ and you hold:

♠ A 8 5 4 3 2   ♡ Q 10   ◇ A 8   ♣ A 6 5

Your 2NT Ogust enquiry fetches a 3◇ reply, showing a minimum hand (6-8 points) and two of the top three honours in hearts. What action should you take?

Dealer South:
Nil vulnerable

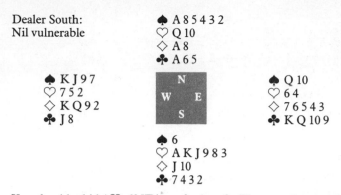

```
                        ♠ A 8 5 4 3 2
                        ♡ Q 10
                        ◇ A 8
                        ♣ A 6 5
    ♠ K J 9 7                              ♠ Q 10
    ♡ 7 5 2            N                    ♡ 6 4
    ◇ K Q 9 2      W       E                ◇ 7 6 5 4 3
    ♣ J 8              S                    ♣ K Q 10 9
                        ♠ 6
                        ♡ A K J 9 8 3
                        ◇ J 10
                        ♣ 7 4 3 2
```

You should rebid 4♡. 3NT is perfectly safe. There are 9 top tricks.
However, there is potential on the North hand for more tricks in hearts.
Perhaps a diamond ruff, perhaps the spades can be set up. As the cards
lie, there is no diamond ruff, but South can score 11 tricks by careful
play, establishing two extra spade winners. Win the diamond lead, cash
♠ A, ruff a spade, heart to the 10, ruff a spade, heart to the queen, ruff a
spade, draw the last trump, cross to dummy's ♣ A and cash the last two
spades.

Dealer North:
Both vulnerable

```
                        ♠ J 4 2
                        ♡ K Q
                        ◇ A K 8 3
                        ♣ A 9 8 6
    ♠ Q 10                                 ♠ K 9 8 7 5 3
    ♡ J 10 7 4 3       N                    ♡ ---
    ◇ 9 4          W       E                ◇ Q 10 7 2
    ♣ K Q J 2          S                    ♣ 7 4 3
                        ♠ A 6
                        ♡ A 9 8 6 5 2
                        ◇ J 6 5
                        ♣ 10 5
```

North opened 1◇, South responded 1♡, North rebid 2NT showing
17-18 points balanced and South ended proceedings with 4♡. 3NT is
also likely to succeed, but in general you should prefer the major suit
game. Here, even if hearts are 3-2, a spade lead could knock out your
entry and prevent your enjoying the hearts. With a long suit and a lack of
outside entries, prefer the suit contract.

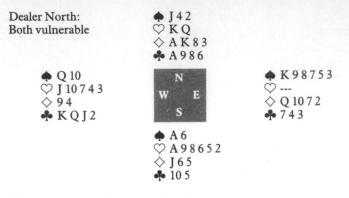

Dealer North:
Both vulnerable

♠ J 4 2
♡ K Q
♢ A K 8 3
♣ A 9 8 6

♠ Q 10
♡ J 10 7 4 3
♢ 9 4
♣ K Q J 2

♠ K 9 8 7 5 3
♡ ---
♢ Q 10 7 2
♣ 7 4 3

♠ A 6
♡ A 9 8 6 5 2
♢ J 6 5
♣ 10 5

(Diagram repeated for convenience)

The suit contract has another advantage. It allows you to deal with a foul break in the trump suit. West led the king of clubs, taken by the ace. The ♡ K revealed the bad news when East signalled with the ♠ 9. South quickly recovered from the shock and led a club to the 10 and jack. West switched to the ♠ Q, won by the ace, and a diamond to dummy's ace was followed by the 9 of clubs on which South discarded a spade. West led a spade ruffed by South who led a heart to the queen, cashed the ♢ K and the ♣ 8 on which South pitched the ♢ J as West had to follow.

South was down to ♡ A-9-8 and West down to ♡ J-10-7. A diamond from dummy was ruffed with the ♡ 8 and West could make only one trump trick. 'Just as well I didn't double,' said West.

With coups like that available, who wants to try for 3NT? Note that 3NT on the actual deal has insoluble problems.

TIP 8

When partner transfers into a major opposite your 1NT opening, you should simply accept the transfer on most hands. Give a super-accept only with 3 out of 3 positive features.

You should be using a transfer structure over 1NT openings. The 1NT : 2 ◇ transfer to hearts and the 1NT : 2 ♡ transfer to spades enable you to bid many more hands accurately than is possible in standard, weakness-takeout methods. Partner's transfer promises at least five cards in the major shown and may be a weak hand (partner intends to pass when you bid the major) or a game-try or game-force hand (partner will bid again to indicate the nature of the hand).

After 1NT : 2 ◇, you should normally bid 2 ♡ (accept) but occasionally your hand will be worth 3 ♡ (a super-accept). The same applies to spades, of course. To super-accept, your hand should have all three positive features in support of partner's major.

The positive features are:

- 4-card support rather than just three.

- Maximum points rather than minimum. If borderline, primary points (aces and kings) rather than secondary points (unsupported queens and jacks).

- A ruffing value via an outside doubleton.

  Suppose you open 1NT, 15-17, and partner bids 2 ♡, a transfer to spades. Which of these is worth a super-accept?

(A) ♠ A K 6 4	(B) ♠ Q 9 7	(C) ♠ K 8 7 4	(D) ♠ 9 6
♡ Q 7	♡ K Q J	♡ A 7	♡ A K 5
◇ K 9 8 3	◇ A K 5	◇ A Q 6 2	◇ K Q J 5
♣ K J 4	♣ Q 7 6 4	♣ A 5 3	♣ A 8 7 2

(A) Bid 2 ♠. You have 4-card support and a doubleton, but your points are borderline and the ♡ Q is of questionable value.

(B) Bid 2 ♠. 17 points, but only 3-card support and no ruffing value.

(C) Bid 3 ♠. Ideal for the super-accept. 4-card support, maximum points, primary honours and a ruffing value.

(D) Bid 2 ♠. No spade support but you are obliged to bid 2 ♠ anyway. You are not permitted to decline the transfer.

The normal way to make a super-accept is to jump to 3-of-the-major-shown. Some pairs use any bid other than 2-of-the-major as a super-accept. In this style, you could use:

2NT = Maximum values, 3/4-card support, 4-3-3-3 pattern and all values outside the major are instant winners. This may enable partner to choose a higher-scoring 3NT.

For example:

WEST	EAST		WEST	EAST
♠ 8 7 2	♠ A 9		1NT	2♢
♡ K 8 6 2	♡ A Q 9 7 5 3		2NT	3NT
♢ A K 4	♢ 9 7 3		No	
♣ A K 5	♣ 9 6			

New suit = Long suit try with 4-card support. The suit bid would typically be J-x-x or J-x-x-x or worse and ask responder whether the losers in that suit could be eliminated.

3-Major = Super accept unsuitable for 2NT or new suit. The theory of the super-accept is that if partner is prepared to play at the 2-level opposite a minimum with only doubleton support, playing at the 3-level with maximum values and 4-card support is not unreasonable. The advantage of the super-accept is that it may encourage partner to bid a game otherwise missed.

After a simple accept, if responder changes suit, this is played as forcing to game. For example:

WEST	EAST
1NT	2♡ = transfer to spades
2♠	3♡ = 4+ hearts, forcing to game
?	

Opener can now support the hearts with 4 trumps, support the spades with 3 trumps or rebid 3NT without support for either major.

If supporting spades, 3♠ is stronger than 4♠. Use 3♠ with 2 out of the 3 positive features mentioned on page 27 and bid 4♠ with only 1 of the positive features. If supporting hearts, 4♡ is the weaker supporting bid, a cue bid of 4♣ or 4♢ shows support for hearts, maximum values (2 or 3 positive features) and the ace in the suit bid.

Suppose the bidding has gone as above. What is opener's rebid with each of these hands? 1NT = 12-14.

(A) ♠ A 8 7 6	(B) ♠ A 8 7 6	(C) ♠ K 5	(D) ♠ K 8 7
♡ K 8 6 3	♡ A 5	♡ K Q 7 5	♡ Q 7 6
♢ 9 7	♢ K J 7 6	♢ A Q 9	♢ A K 9 3
♣ K Q 2	♣ 7 6 2	♣ 7 6 4 2	♣ 8 7 3

(A)   Bid 4♡. You have support for spades and hearts but should give precedence to the 4-4 fit (*see* Tip 5).

(B)   Bid 3♠. You have excellent spade support (positive feature 1) and a doubleton heart (ruffing value, positive feature 2). Therefore give the stronger preference. This may help partner if partner has any slam ambitions. Partner knows you cannot have 3/3 positive features as you did not super-accept over 2♡.

(C)   Bid 4 $\diamondsuit$. This shows support for hearts, maximum values and the ace of diamonds. Your hand could hardly be better for hearts.

(D)   Bid 4 $\spadesuit$. You have spade preference but your hand is very weak. Minimum values, only 3-card support 4-3-3-3 pattern and so no ruffing value. 4 $\spadesuit$ will tend to dampen any enthusiasm partner may have for slam. Do not consider rebidding 3NT. Partner's hand is at least 5-4 in the majors and partner need not have any significant holding in clubs at all.

TIP 9

After a 1NT or 2NT bid, do not introduce a minor suit into a game-forcing auction unless you have slam ambitions.

Since pairs strategy involves not playing in a minor suit game, it is best to gamble on 3NT if you have game values, no major suit and no slam ambitions. If you have a major, by all means explore the major suit game but do not suggest a minor suit to partner.

If partner opens 1NT, 12-14, each of these hands would be worth 3NT and not a minor suit bid in a standard approach.

(A) ♠ A 6	(B) ♠ 9 5	(C) ♠ 6	(D) ♠ A 4 2
♡ 6 5	♡ 6 3	♡ A 6	♡ 8
◇ K Q 8 7 6	◇ A K Q 9 7 4	◇ K J 9 6 5	◇ A J 2
♣ A 4 3 2	♣ K 8 3	♣ A 9 6 4 2	♣ K J 10 8 7 4

Risky? Of course, but what do you want? Safety or winning? What you do desperately need when you bid 3NT on such hands is a sympathetic partner who will not rebuke you if the gamble does not come off.

Some partnerships have introduced splinter jumps over 1NT, so that on hands (C) and (D) they would bid 1NT : 3 ♠ and 1NT : 3 ♡ to show a shortage in the suit bid and checking that partner does have the suit stopped. That approach is a long way yet from standard and requires adjustments to other parts of your system.

It follows that auctions like 1NT : 3 ♣ or 1NT : 3 ◇ or 2NT : 3 ◇ when used in a natural sense at pairs carry a slam suggestion. Accordingly, opener should not be reluctant to give 3-card or better support. An immediate cue bid (e.g. 1NT : 3 ◇, 3 ♠) would show support for the minor and an ace in the suit bid, while raising the minor (1NT : 3 ◇, 4 ◇) would show support but deny an outside ace.

Another avant-garde approach here is to show key cards in support of the minor, as with Roman Key Card Blackwood. For example after 1NT : 3 ♣—

3NT = only doubleton support or 3 rags and minimum values.

All other actions show support—

3 ◇ = 0 or 3 key cards
3 ♡ = 1 or 4 key cards (4 not possible for a 12-14 1NT)
3 ♠ = 2 key cards, no trump queen
4 ♣ = 2 key cards + trump queen

Naturally you would need to settle this with partner in advance.

The same philosophy applies if you transfer in reply to 1NT or 2NT. Do not rebid with a change of suit into a minor unless you have slam ambitions. For example:

WEST   East opens 1NT, 12-14, and West transfers via 2♡
♠ A J 9 7 3   showing the 5 spades. East bids 2♠. What next?
♡ 7
◇ K Q 7   Best is 3NT, offering partner the choice between 4♠
♣ K 8 5 4   and 3NT. The trap to avoid is 3♣. You will not be
                pleased to hear partner bid 4♣. Of course, the ideal
rebid would be 3 No-hearts, but that is not allowed as yet.

Failure to adhere to this principle cost dearly on the following deal:

Dealer East: ♠ J 7 6
Both vulnerable   ♡ 7 6 4 2
                ◇ A 5
                ♣ A K 7 3

♠ Q 10 8 5 3   ♠ A K 2
♡ A 9   ♡ K J 10
◇ J 10 9 3   ◇ K Q 7 6 4
♣ 9 4   ♣ Q 6

                ♠ 9 4
                ♡ Q 8 5 3
                ◇ 8 2
                ♣ J 10 8 5 2

The actual bidding went:

WEST	EAST
	1NT(1)
2♡(2)	2NT(3)
3◇	4◇
4♠	4NT
No	

(1)   15-18
(2)   Transfer to spades
(3)   This showed a super-accept for spades.

Over 2NT, West should have bid 4♠ without further ado. The
introduction of the diamond suit is a mystery. East naturally supported
and West tried to bail out in 4♠. You cannot blame East for reading
West's sequence as slam inviting, otherwise West would have bid 4♠ at
once over 2NT. East's hand looks ideal for a slam in diamonds or spades
even opposite a borderline slam invitation. When East followed through
with 4NT, West in desperation passed.

The pair involved were no rank amateurs. The hand arose in the 1989
World Championships won by Brazil and the above sequence was
produced by a pair from that Brazilian team. If it could happen to them,
it could happen to anyone. A copy of this tip has been despatched to
them post haste.

TIP 10

If partner opens 1♡ or 1♠ and you have support, but a balanced hand with 10 losers, choose a 1NT response rather than a raise to 2♡/2♠.

This is particularly important for pairs using 5-card majors or 5-card 1♠ openings, but is also relevant for pairs playing 4-card openings. These hands typify the sort which are unsuitable for an immediate raise of 1♠ to 2♠:

(A) ♠ K 8 7	(B) ♠ A 5 3	(C) ♠ 8 6 4 3	(D) ♠ 9 7 5
♡ A 8 7	♡ J 7	♡ K Q J	♡ Q 7 6 2
◇ 9 8 7 3	◇ J 8 6 3	◇ 8 7 6	◇ K 8 6 3
♣ 7 6 2	♣ 8 7 5 4	♣ 7 4 2	♣ J 7

These hands all have sufficient point count to warrant a raise to 2♠, but a 1NT response will provide a better result most of the time. Responding 1NT certainly runs a risk—you may be left to play 1NT—but to raise to 2♠ runs an even greater risk. Partner plays you for the normal equivalent for the 2♠ raise, about 6-9 points and 8-9 losers. If you respond 2♠ and partner takes further action, you are almost certainly headed for a minus result.

If you respond 2♠, partner is enthusiastic to take action. The raise spurs partner on. In addition, if the opponents compete, partner is quick to compete over them at the 3-level. This again is likely to produce an unwelcome result because your hand is so short of tricks.

If you respond 1NT, a number of good things can happen. If you are left to play in 1NT, you may find that you achieve a respectable score. On some days you may actually make 1NT when 2♠ would have failed. Even if you go minus, perhaps your contract fails by fewer tricks than 2♠ would. Perhaps your 1NT inhibits opposition competition and they have a partscore available which would gain them more than your loss in 1NT.

If partner does not pass 1NT, partner may rebid in another suit and you might locate a better fit. On Hand D, for example, if opener rebids 2♡ over your 1NT, you have certainly done better than if you had raised to 2♠.

If partner rebids in another suit and your preference is for spades, you simply revert to 2♠. This auction has a huge advantage for your side. The sound of the auction is that your preference to spades is reluctant and you may not hold genuine support at all. Indeed, you may have given a preference on a mere doubleton. The opponents now are less likely to compete and you may buy the contract in 2♠. In other words, 1♠ : 2♠, Pass invites competition, while opponents are far more reluctant to push higher against auctions like 1♠ : 1NT, 2♣ : 2♠. They often find in those auctions that they have three losers each in opener's major.

Another advantage to the 1NT response arises when opener rebids the major over your 1NT. After 1 ♠ : 1NT, 2 ♠ you will naturally pass on each of the above hands and again you are quite likely to buy the auction in 2 ♠. There is no inkling on the auction that you have a strong trump fit. The spade fit could be 6-1. The opponents will be far more reluctant to compete against 1 ♠ : 1NT, 2 ♠ than against 1 ♠ : 2 ♠, Pass.

Further, if the bidding were to start 1 ♠ : 2 ♠ and opener has the length required for 1 ♠ : 1NT, 2 ♠ then opener will not sell out to the opposition if they compete over 2 ♠. Opener is almost a certainty to push on to 3 ♠ or perhaps take a gamble with 4 ♠. Your hand will not be met with squeals of elation.

Those who use the '1NT Forcing' response have been using this approach for years, raising to 2 ♠ on sound values and taking a delayed raise on the 10-loser (or worse) hands by replying 1NT first. Those among us who do not fancy the 1NT-Forcing gadget can still adopt the same strategy.

Of course, there will be the occasional losses by responding 1NT in this situation, but in the long run, I'm prepared to wager that the upside results will significantly outscore the downside potential.

PART 2: COMPETITIVE BIDDING

In no other area of match-pointed pairs are the rewards so great for a sound approach. Time and time again you will find that the winners are not those who can bid brilliantly to a fine grand slam missed by the field or those who can play an exotic squeeze successfully. No, the winners come from those who are able to judge the right time to push, the right time to defend, how high to go, when to double.

Judgment here brings in the matchpoints but so does a sound systemic strategy for pairs. Many players find it difficult to throw off the shackles of rubber bridge in this area. Many remain wedded (or welded) to the penalty double. At low levels particularly, the frequency and usefulness of takeout doubles relegates the penalty double to the dinosaur era in the evolution of competitive bidding. Competitive doubles do not mean that penalties cannot be collected, but they do entail the recognition that takeout doubles have far greater flexibility and usefulness. At pairs, frequency of success counts, not the size of the score. When that factor is appreciated, the partnership will adopt low level takeout doubles in countless areas previously the domain of the penalty double.

Basic strategy for contesting the partscore includes the following:

- Pushing from the 2-level to the 3-level when their side has a trump fit or when your side has a trump fit and their auction has subsided at the 2 level.
- Competing above them at the 3-level only when you hold at least 9 trumps or some other significant additional feature.
- Not competing to the 4-level on merely partscore values.

The following tips for competitive auctions will supplement your basic strategy.

TIP 11

Adopt a style where any double by the partnership at the 1-level or 2-level of a suit bid is primarily for takeout, whether by opener or by responder or by either partner of the defending side.

This approach will allow both partners to compete freely with a double which promises no strength beyond what was originally promised. In summary:

1. A double of 1NT or 2NT is for penalties. (Exception: Double in the sequence—1X : No : 1NT : Double . . . is a takeout double of suit X.)

2. A double after a penalty redouble—1♠ : Dble : Rdble . . . is for penalties, as the redouble intimated the desire for penalties.

3. A double is for penalties after a previous takeout double has been passed for penalties. For example:

WEST	NORTH	EAST	SOUTH
1♢	2♣	Dble	No
No	2♡	Dble . . .	

East's first double was for takeout (a negative double but better termed a 'responder's double') but East's second double is for penalties, as West's pass converted the original double to penalties.

4. *All Other Doubles at the 1-Level and 2-Level are for Takeout.*

Suppose the bidding has been:

WEST	NORTH	EAST	SOUTH
1♠	No	1NT	2♣
?			

What action should West take with:

♠ A 10 9 8 4   ♡ A K 7   ♢ J 7 4 3   ♣ 3

The complete deal from a world championship in the 1950s looked like this:

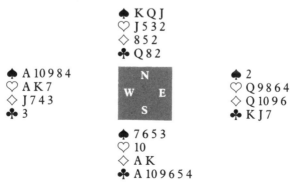

```
                    ♠ K Q J
                    ♡ J 5 3 2
                    ♢ 8 5 2
                    ♣ Q 8 2
  ♠ A 10 9 8 4                        ♠ 2
  ♡ A K 7            N                ♡ Q 9 8 6 4
  ♢ J 7 4 3        W   E              ♢ Q 10 9 6
  ♣ 3                S                ♣ K J 7
                    ♠ 7 6 5 3
                    ♡ 10
                    ♢ A K
                    ♣ A 10 9 6 5 4
```

At the table West (Konstam) passed 2 ♣ and so did East (Schapiro). 10 tricks were made. At the other table, South did not bid and East-West played in 3 ◇ and made 9 tricks.

Today, no one would pass the South cards. Over 2 ♣, West should double. Note that this promises no extra strength, simply a shortage in clubs and a desire to compete in any of the other three suits. This enables the heart fit to be found, a difficult task if South fails to bid. In reply to the double, East could afford to bid 3 ♡ which West would pass.

If West had a hand suitable to penalise 2 ♣, West would pass. East is expected to compete if possible and the primary choice would be a takeout double. This allows West to pass and convert it to penalties.

Do not be dismayed if you do not catch every penalty. Even if you scored no low level penalties, the competitive takeout double will find the best contract for you so often, you will not begrudge other competitors their use of the penalty double weapon (a Stone Age tool by today's standards).

Where responder has bid a major at the 1-level, opener can utilise the double to indicate 3-card support. Suppose the bidding has started:

WEST	NORTH	EAST	SOUTH
1 ◇	No	1 ♡	1 ♠
?			

What should West do on each of these hands?

(A) ♠ 9	(B) ♠ 96	(C) ♠ 9	(D) ♠ 96
♡ Q 7 4	♡ Q 7 4 2	♡ Q 7 4	♡ 8 2
◇ A J 8 6 3	◇ A K 9 6 3	◇ A K J 6 5 2	◇ A Q J 7 6 2
♣ A Q 7 2	♣ K J	♣ A K 3	♣ A J 4

Solutions: (A)   Double. Ideal. Tolerance for hearts, support for the other suits. Do not worry about the minimum values. The shape justifies action.

(B)   Bid 2 ♡. A benefit of the double is that the raise guarantees 4-card support. With only 3 hearts, you would double. This is a huge edge for later competition compared with those pairs who have to guess whether the raise was based on 3 trumps or 4 trumps.

(C)   Double. If partner bids 2 ♡, you will raise. If partner rebids 1NT or 2 ♣, it is time enough then to jump to 3 ◇.

(D)   2 ◇. Another advantage of the competitive double is that when you fail to double you will not hold 3-card support for responder's major. In this auction, East will know that West has at most two hearts.

TIP 12

Where opener has bid two suits and responder's rebid is preference back to the first suit at the 2-level, bid in the direct seat as though you were in fourth seat. The same applies if opener's rebid was 1NT and responder rebids by supporting opener's suit at the 2-level.

You should treat this situation for South:

WEST	NORTH	EAST	SOUTH
1♦	No	1♠	No
2♣	No	2♦	?

in the same way as this situation for North:

WEST	NORTH	EAST	SOUTH
1♦	No	1♠	No
2♣	No	2♦	No
No	?		

In the pass-out seat, North will strive to compete but will need some reasonable holding in the unbid suit. If North's shape is 4-3-3-3 or 4-4-3-2 with length in their suits, North will usually be hamstrung. When East gives weak preference, there is a risk that the auction is about to die out. You therefore must take the risk of bidding in the direct seat.

Suppose the bidding has been as above up to East's 2♦. What action should South take with:

♠ A 4 3   ♡ A K 8 7 3   ◇ 8 2   ♣ 10 8 6

On the actual deal, North-South paid the price for ineffectual competitive spirit and West did well as declarer:

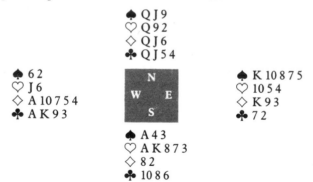

```
              ♠ Q J 9
              ♡ Q 9 2
              ◇ Q J 6
              ♣ Q J 5 4
♠ 6 2                        ♠ K 10 8 7 5
♡ J 6          N             ♡ 10 5 4
◇ A 10 7 5 4  W   E          ◇ K 9 3
♣ A K 9 3      S             ♣ 7 2
              ♠ A 4 3
              ♡ A K 8 7 3
              ◇ 8 2
              ♣ 10 8 6
```

$2\diamondsuit$ was passed out and North led the 2 of hearts. West ruffed the third round of hearts and recognised the problem in continuing with three rounds of clubs (no convenient return to hand). At trick 4 a spade was led: jack, king, ace. The club return was taken by the ace and West led another spade, taken by the queen.

The rest was now easy. West won the next club, cashed the ace and king of diamonds and ran the spades. North won the $\diamondsuit$ Q but West had eight tricks.

Of course, South should have bid $2\heartsuit$ over $2\diamondsuit$. Even if the defence starts with $\clubsuit$ A, $\clubsuit$ K, club ruff, diamond to the ace, club ruffed and overruffed, declarer is home in $2\heartsuit$ via the spade finesse and discarding a spade on an established diamond winner. The best then that East-West can do is bid $3\diamondsuit$ for one down. Either way, South obtains a plus and a respectable matchpoint score.

Yes, $2\heartsuit$ is risky. West might be very strong. West or East might be able to double $2\heartsuit$. So what? To pass $2\diamondsuit$ is not risk free as the above has shown. To enjoy success, you must be prepared to court failure. True in life, true at the bridge table.

The same philosophy applies if opener rebids 1NT in auctions such as:

WEST	NORTH	EAST	SOUTH
$1\diamondsuit$	No	$1\spadesuit$	No
1NT	No	$2\diamondsuit$	?

What action should South take with:

$\spadesuit$ A 8 6 3 $\heartsuit$ K 9 8 3 $\diamondsuit$ 6 $\clubsuit$ Q 10 7 5

South should treat bidding in this direct seat just as though it were in the pass-out seat, as for North after:

WEST	NORTH	EAST	SOUTH
$1\diamondsuit$	No	$1\spadesuit$	No
1NT	No	$2\diamondsuit$	No
No	?		

It is even more important to bid in an auction such as this. Here the diamond support will be genuine and East-West are sure to have at least an 8-card fit. In the earlier auctions where a mere preference was involved, the opponent's 8-card fit is not assured.

On the given hand, South should double $2\diamondsuit$, for takeout of course (*see* Tip 11). South's failure to act on the previous round will dampen any enthusiasm North might feel. Importantly, the best contract for North-South could be in spades. The response of 1-Major can be in a worthless 4-card suit.

TIP 13

When making a negative double with 10-12 points, the hand pattern will normally be 4-4-3-2 or 4-3-3-3. A 4-4-4-1 pattern is a slight possibility.

When you have 10 HCP or more and a 5-card or longer suit, you can usually develop the hand in a natural way, starting by bidding your long suit. Your high card values and suit length will justify a change of suit at the 2-level.

♠ A J 8 7   Partner opens 1♢ and next player bids 1♡. Bid 2♣
♡ 7   rather than double or 1♠. You are strong enough to
♢ K 7 4   rebid 2♠ if partner comes back with 2♢ or if the
♣ K 9 8 4 2   opponents compete with 2♡, passed back to you.

It follows that if you double first and change suit on the next round, your hand will be weak, in the 6-9 point range. The change of suit will be a 5-card suit at least. Why then did you double and not simply bid the 5-card suit? Because your hand was not strong enough for that sequence. For example:

♠ 9   Partner opens 1♣ and RHO bids 1♠. You double
♡ Q J 7 3   and partner rebids 1NT. You now rebid 2♢,
♢ K 10 9 6 4 2 showing at least 5 diamonds and logically a weak hand
♣ 8 6   as you failed to respond 2♢ initially. If LHO bids
               2♠ and this is passed back to you, you will compete
with 3♢. You should not pass it out at the 2-level (basic partscore strategy when they have a trump fit) and partner will not read you for a strong hand as you failed to respond 2♢ in the first instance.

Having made a negative double with 10-12 points you will usually take a second action over a minimum rebid by opener. Your second action will be 2NT or raising opener to the 3-level. There will rarely be any other option, given that your hand patterns are so limited.

Suppose the bidding has started:

WEST	NORTH	EAST	SOUTH
1♢	1♠	Dble	No
2♣	No	?	

What action should East now take with these hands?

(A) ♠ K 7 5	(B) ♠ 10 7	(C) ♠ 3 2	(D) ♠ 7 6 2
♡ J 7 3 2	♡ A 8 5 2	♡ K J 6 3	♡ A 8 6 2
♢ A 6 4	♢ J 4 3	♢ A J 6 5	♢ K 8 7
♣ K 8 7	♣ A Q 8 2	♣ Q 9 6	♣ K J 4

Solutions: (A)   Rebid 2NT. Shows 10-12 points and a stopper in spades. Enables opener to pass, raise to 3NT or revert to a minor.

(B)   Raise to 3♣. Shows 10-12 points and club support. Implies no stopper in spades. With club support and a spade stopper and balanced shape, 2NT would be preferred.

(C)   Rebid with 3♢. Shows 10-12 points and diamond support and, as for B, implies no spade stopper.

(D)   Rebid with 3♢. Not hugely attractive, but better than the other choices. Much too strong for 2♢ and 2NT is out with no spade cover.

WEST	EAST	WEST	NORTH	EAST	SOUTH
♠ K 5 3	♠ 8 2	No	No	1♣	1♠
♡ K Q 9 6	♡ A 3	Dble	No	2♣	No
♢ K 8 4	♢ Q 7 2	2NT	No	3♣	No
♣ 7 4 2	♣ K Q J 9 6 5	No	No		

West shows an invitational hand with spades stopped. East has no more than partscore ambitions and should therefore choose the normal partscore, clubs.

WEST	EAST	WEST	NORTH	EAST	SOUTH
♠ 8 4 2	♠ A 9	1♡	1♠	Dble	No
♡ A J 9 4 3	♡ 8 5	2♣	No	2NT	No
♢ K 6	♢ A 7 5 3 2	No	No		
♣ K J 6	♣ Q 10 8 4				

When showing two suits with the double (both majors or both minors), a 5-4 pattern is quite acceptable. Here the double to show diamonds *and* clubs works better than to bid 2♢, although East is certainly worth 2♢. Asked to pick a minor, West obliges with 2♣. East is worth one more try and chooses 2NT. This is a better shot than 3♣. West already knows East has 4 clubs and can revert to 3♣ if 2NT does not appeal. As it is, West is delighted to leave 2NT in.

As responder will take second action with 10 points or more, opener need not become too excited opposite a negative double on nice-looking minimum openings. If opener needs 10 points opposite in order to have a decent chance for game, it is enough to make a minimum rebid. Responder will oblige if the 10 points or more are indeed there.

If opener does jump in reply to the double, opener is asking responder to bid game if at the top end of the 6-9 minimum range. Opener should have about 17-18 points for the jump rebid and responder should bid on with 8-9 points and pass only with 6-7.

If opener has enough for game opposite 6-7 points, opener should simply bid game. If unsure of the best game, bid the enemy suit.

TIP 14

After a negative double by responder, opener should not compete to the 3-level in the direct seat with just minimum values.

In auctions such as these:

WEST	NORTH	EAST	SOUTH
1 $\diamondsuit$	1 $\spadesuit$	Dble	2 $\spadesuit$
?			

opener should pass with a minimum opening and bid 3 $\heartsuit$, 3 $\diamondsuit$ or 3 $\clubsuit$ only with extra values, around the 16-18 mark. This will enable responder to gauge opener's strength. Pass will deny 16 points and a bid will show the extra. Otherwise, if opener bids here willy-nilly, responder will find it tough to decide whether to bid on if responder has more than a bare minimum.

What should 'Double' by opener here mean? It is for takeout and indicates 16-18 points, but without any clearcut bid. A holding of three hearts only would be part of the expectation. The rest will vary according to the contents of your system.

It is safe to pass on a decent minimum hand, even with four hearts, since, assuming your partner understands basic competitive strategy, the bidding will not die out at 2 $\spadesuit$. Partner can compete with 3 $\clubsuit$ (5-card suit), 3 $\diamondsuit$ (4-card support), 3 $\heartsuit$ (6-card suit or excellent 5-carder) or another double, if no other action is attractive.

For example, suppose the bidding has gone as above and West and North have passed. What action should East take on these hands?

(A) $\spadesuit$ 8 7 6	(B) $\spadesuit$ 8 7	(C) $\spadesuit$ 6 3	(D) $\spadesuit$ 6 3
$\heartsuit$ K Q 6 3	$\heartsuit$ K 9 7 6	$\heartsuit$ Q J 10 6 5 2	$\heartsuit$ Q J 4 2
$\diamondsuit$ Q 9 8 4	$\diamondsuit$ 5 4	$\diamondsuit$ K 3	$\diamondsuit$ Q 9 8
$\clubsuit$ 8 7	$\clubsuit$ A J 8 4 3	$\clubsuit$ 8 4 2	$\clubsuit$ K 5 4 2

Solutions: (A) Bid 3 $\diamondsuit$. Opener knows you have 4 hearts from the double and can give preference to 3 $\heartsuit$.

(B) Bid 3 $\clubsuit$. This implies 5 clubs and 4 hearts and fewer than 3 diamonds. With 3 diamonds as well, it would be better to double again.

(C) Bid 3 $\heartsuit$. You were too weak for 2 $\heartsuit$ over 1 $\spadesuit$, but the suit warrants 3 $\heartsuit$. Partner will know your hand is not robust because of the failure to bid 2 $\heartsuit$ on the first round.

(D) Double. You must not sell out to 2 $\spadesuit$, but who knows which spot is best? Hopefully partner will. The second double is still for takeout, of course.

How should the bidding go on this deal, North-South using a 15-17 1NT opening?

Dealer South:
Nil vulnerable

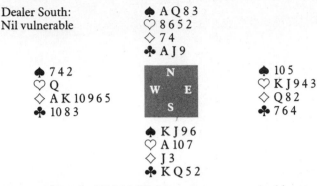

♠ A Q 8 3
♡ 8 6 5 2
◇ 7 4
♣ A J 9

♠ 7 4 2
♡ Q
◇ A K 10 9 6 5
♣ 10 8 3

♠ 10 5
♡ K J 9 4 3
◇ Q 8 2
♣ 7 6 4

♠ K J 9 6
♡ A 10 7
◇ J 3
♣ K Q 5 2

The deal from the USA highlights a common error in this area.

WEST	NORTH	EAST	SOUTH
			1♣
2◇ (1)	Dble(2)	3◇	3♠
No	4♠	All pass	

(1)   Weak jump overcall

(2)   Responder's takeout, promises both majors

This is a foolish game with two losers in each red suit. You cannot blame North for bidding on. South might have been much better for the 3♠ bid. The error was South's for that 3♠ bid which should be in the 16-18 range. The auction ought to go:

WEST	NORTH	EAST	SOUTH
			1♣
2◇	Dble	3◇	No
No	Dble	No	?

This competitive double indicates a hand in the 10-12 zone. With most 6-9 point hands, North would pass 3◇. In reply to the second double, South would do best to pass, as 3◇ doubled can go for −300. If South does bid, 3♠ is enough and the silly 4♠ will be avoided.

The play was a contest in missed chances. West cashed two diamonds and switched to a trump. (The switch to the ♡Q is not difficult on the actual auction. Where else could the tricks come from?) Declarer drew trumps, East pitching a heart, and cashed four rounds of clubs, East pitching another heart.

The position now was:

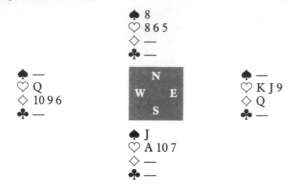

Declarer now did well by leading the ♡7 to West's queen. If East ducked this, declarer would come home via the forced ruff and sluff. East did best by overtaking with the ♡K and returning the ♡9. Declarer should have made by finessing the ♡10, but rose with the ♡A and went one off. If West had Q-J bare, why would East overtake? Rising with the ace also played for East to have started with ♡K-9-4-3. That would give East 4 diamonds (and West only 5 diamonds for the weak jump). If so, East could safely discard the diamonds rather than shorten the hearts. At least justice was served for South's 3♠ bid.

TIP 15

If the hand does not belong to your side, do not make a penalty double at the 2-level or 3-level without a trump stack and a misfit with partner's hand.

At pairs, there is a tendency to make light penalty doubles at low levels, particularly if the opponents are vulnerable. This is attractive because if it goes sour and the opponents make it, it is only one board, about 4% of your total session score. As each board counts equally, an utter catastrophe which produces a bottom board is no worse than a most modest error which produces a bottom score. A bottom is a bottom—at pairs the size of the bottom is irrelevant.*

The second attraction is that if you can defeat them by one trick when they are vulnerable, your score of +200 should be a top, outscoring any other normal partscore result.

Nevertheless, against a competent declarer it does not pay to double at a low level if the high card strength is roughly equal. A surprising trump stack and a misfit with partner are the hallmarks for a successful low level penalty. Without them, it does not pay to double unless you have a clearcut superiority in high card strength, say 23-17 or 24-16. Then the hand belongs to your side and you could reasonably expect a decent plus score. Therefore you double to retrieve that score.

When the points are about equally divided and each side has a trump fit, each side can usually make 8 tricks. If one side has 9 trumps, then one side can often make 9 tricks. Which side it is will depend on which side's finesses are working. A finesse that works for one side is a finesse that fails when the other side is playing the contract. As you cannot see in the bidding which way these key finesses will work, it is better to steer away from low-level penalty doubles when the points are about even or the opponent's way.

On borderline hands, you will do well enough if you defeat their contract and achieve a plus. If you can be plus most of the time on the marginal hands, your matchpoint score will be excellent without having to take any daredevil risks.

Suppose partner has opened a weak $2\heartsuit$. The opponents compete with $2\spadesuit$, you push to $3\heartsuit$ and they compete again with $3\spadesuit$. What action should you take with:

$\spadesuit$ K 10 7 $\heartsuit$ A 5 4 $\diamondsuit$ Q 8 4 2 $\clubsuit$ 5 3 2

---

*The possible puns in this area are almost limitless.

The deal arose in the first officially recognized duplicate in the USSR, in Leningrad, October 1989. The winners were Oppenheim–Witek of Poland, while the runners-up were Bulgaria's Trendafilov–Ivanov who gained heavily as a result of an unsound double.

Dealer South:
North-South vulnerable

♠ Q J 5 4
♡ 6 2
◇ J 9 7 5
♣ A 7 6

♠ 6 2
♡ K Q J 10 8 3
◇ 10 6
♣ K Q 4

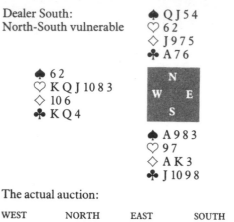

♠ K 10 7
♡ A 5 4
◇ Q 8 4 2
♣ 5 3 2

♠ A 9 8 3
♡ 9 7
◇ A K 3
♣ J 10 9 8

The actual auction:

WEST	NORTH	EAST	SOUTH
			No (1)
2♡ (2)	No	No	2♠ (3)
No	No	3♡	No
No	3♠ (4)	Dble (5)	All pass

(1)   In the 'decadent West', three quick tricks are enough for an opening bid. Most 12-point hands should be opened.

(2)   Super-strong for a weak two. 1♡ would be the most common action.

(3)   Double for takeout would be the universal expert choice in the West.

(4)   No doubt expecting at least a 5-card suit with South. Even then, North should pass. Opposite a hand that could not open, North cannot reasonably expect to make 3♠ with such a balanced hand. Most of the time 3♠ will fail and 3♡ may well fail, too. At the 3-level, both sides are often in jeopardy. Choose to defend.

(5)   No doubt East was influenced by the vulnerability and the fact that South was unable to open the bidding. Nevertheless, all the signs were there to show that the double was wrong. Too much of a fit with partner (either opponent might have had a singleton heart), no trump stack and not enough points. Even opposite a 1♡ opening, it would be foolish to double as the hand does not clearly belong to your side. Opposite a weak 2♡, it was suicidal—even though the double nearly came off.

West led the ♠ 6 to the jack, king, ace. A spade was returned to the queen and a heart led. East rose with ♡ A and cashed the ♠ 10, followed by a low heart taken by West. The ♣ K shift was won in dummy and declarer came to hand with a diamond to continue with a deceptive ♣ 9 (hoping West might duck and fall victim to an endplay later). West took the ♣ Q and exited with the third club.

South now knew West had at most 2 diamonds and the points revealed by West meant the ◇ Q was with East. Therefore declarer ruffed his 13th club in dummy and led the ◇ J, pinning the 10. That old bridge adage was proved right again: the pin is mightier than the axe.

TIP 16

Don't put all your eggs in one basket. Use the competitive double freely to maximise your options.

(1) The bidding has been:

Dealer West:	WEST	NORTH	EAST	SOUTH
Both vulnerable	1♡	2♢	No	No
	?			

What action should West take with:

♠ A 7 6
♡ A K 9 6 4 2
♢ 7
♣ Q 8 4

(2) The bidding has been:

Dealer North:	WEST	NORTH	EAST	SOUTH
Nil vulnerable	No	No	1♠	
	Dble	2♠	No	No
	?			

What action should West take with:

♠ 6 2
♡ K 9 8 5
♢ A K J 7 6 2
♣ A

(3) The bidding has been:

Dealer North:	WEST	NORTH	EAST	SOUTH
Nil vulnerable	No	No	1♠	
	Dble	2♢	No	No
	2♡	2♠	No	No
	?			

What action should West take with:

♠ A
♡ A Q 10 8 5 2
♢ A 8
♣ K 9 7 4

Solutions: (1) Many players would re-open the bidding with 2♡. This is exactly the error of putting all your eggs in one basket. Yes, the hearts are strong, but the best trump suit is the one where the partnership has the most cards, not your personal best. 2♡ could be the best spot but partner could hold any of these hands:

(A) ♠ Q 9 8 4 2   (B) ♠ 8 5 2   (C) ♠ K 5 4
    ♡ 7   ♡ 7   ♡ 7
    ♢ 8 6 5 2   ♢ J 10 2   ♢ K Q 9 6 2
    ♣ K 5 3   ♣ K J 7 5 3 2 ♣ 9 7 5 2

If you bid 2♡, partner is likely to pass each time (partner may try 2NT with (C), yet the best spot is 2♠ on (A), 3♣ on (B), and 2♢ doubled on (C). How will you reach these spots except by doubling?

(2) Many players would be seduced by the suit texture into a 3♢ bid and that could be the best spot. Nevertheless, bidding 3♢ may also miss your optimal contract. If you do bid 3♢, what do you expect partner to do with:

♠ J 9 7   ♡ Q 10 7 6 3   ♢ 5 4   ♣ J 8 6

Partner will pass 3♢ because the sequence you have chosen, double followed by new suit, implies a 1-suited hand, a hand too strong for an immediate overcall. That is exactly how you would bid if you held:

♠ A 2   ♡ 9 4   ♢ A K J 7 6 2 ♣ K Q 3

The solution is that West should double 2♠. If partner bids 3♡, fine. If East bids 3♣, then and only then should you bid your 3♢.

(3) West should double. Partner has heard the auction, has heard you bid 2♡, has heard the opponents bid spades and diamonds and so should be able to make a sensible decision. There is no reasonable interpretation for the double other than you want partner to take action because you are uncertain of the best action.

The hand arose in the 1989 European Championships and the double eluded the competitors. If you passed 2♠, you have done well, for the opponents are in a 4-2 fit. If you double, you have done better. Partner with six trumps will know what to do even though your double is for takeout. It would be remarkable if North-South could salvage the position and land in 3♣, their best spot.

If you decided to bid 3♣ or 3♡, you will have to play brilliantly to achieve a plus score. On Vugraph, the actual West rescued North-South from 2♠ (which was cold for East-West) into 3♣ (which was cold for North-South). Competitive doubles, anyone?

TIP 17

After an opponent has opened 1NT and opener's partner has made a weakness takeout, be reluctant to let them play in that trump suit at the 2-level and be prepared to compete to the 3-level. If their sequence involves a transfer response, take competitive action only in the pass-out seat, not in the direct seat (as responder may yet have a strong hand).

Where the bidding has started:

WEST	NORTH	EAST	SOUTH
1NT	No	2♡ . . .	

both South and North should compete on suitable values if 2♡ is a natural weak response.

If 2♡ is a transfer to spades, both North and South should wait for the bidding to go:

WEST	NORTH	EAST	SOUTH
1NT	No	2♡	No
2♠	No	No	?

Now South should find some action if at all possible.

It is risky to bid in this position. At rubber bridge the danger of a huge loss has an inhibiting effect. At pairs, the size of the loss is not as important as the frequency.

The weakness takeout after 1NT should be treated in almost the same way as auctions which start:

WEST	NORTH	EAST	SOUTH
1♠	No	2♠	No
No	?		

It is risky to bid but riskier to pass. You could be in trouble if you bid but you are more likely handing them a good score if you leave them at the 2-level.

The weakness takeout may be only a 7-card fit, but some of the time the responder has a 6-card suit and a lot of the time, the opener has 3-card support. When they have an 8-card fit, your strategy should be not to let them play at the 2-level. Take the risk.

Suppose the bidding has been:

Dealer West:	WEST	NORTH	EAST	SOUTH
North-South vulnerable	1NT	No	2♡	No
	2♠	No	No	?

1NT = 12-14. 2♡ = transfer to spades

What action should South take with:

(A) ♠ 7 6　　(B) ♠ 8　　(C) ♠ 10 7 5
　　♡ K 6　　　　♡ A 9 5 2　　　♡ A 7
　　◇ A J 7 6　　◇ K Q 6 3　　　◇ A K J 7 6
　　♣ Q 10 9 5 2　♣ J 10 8 3　　　♣ 8 6 2

Solutions: (A) Bid 2NT, unusual for the minors. If you do not already have that agreement with your partners, settle it soon. It would be unwise to bid 3 ♣ when partner may have a better fit for the diamonds (don't put all your eggs in one basket). You cannot afford to double as partner would probably reply in hearts.

(B) Double. The ideal hand. Yes, you are vulnerable. Yes, it may cost. What are you, man or mouse? Squeak up.

(C) Bid 3 ◇. You have no second suit of interest and therefore no takeout action is suitable. What you need to bid 3 ◇ is courage. The deal arose in the 1989 Far East Pairs:

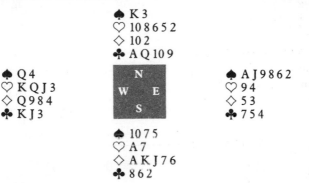

　　　　　　　♠ K 3
　　　　　　　♡ 10 8 6 5 2
　　　　　　　◇ 10 2
　　　　　　　♣ A Q 10 9

♠ Q 4　　　　　　　　　　　♠ A J 9 8 6 2
♡ K Q J 3　　　　　　　　　♡ 9 4
◇ Q 9 8 4　　　　　　　　　◇ 5 3
♣ K J 3　　　　　　　　　　♣ 7 5 4

　　　　　　　♠ 10 7 5
　　　　　　　♡ A 7
　　　　　　　◇ A K J 7 6
　　　　　　　♣ 8 6 2

As it happens, 2 ♠ can be defeated by two tricks by careful defence, even though East-West have an 8-card fit. The club position is the critical one. Where one side's finesses lose, they work for the other side in their contract.

Declarer also managed to make 3 ◇ by careful play despite having only seven trumps. The ♡ K was led, won by South who led a spade to the king and ace. Once East turned up with the ♠ A, declarer was able to place most of the remaining high cards.

East switched to a trump, taken by the ace. A heart went to West's jack and West continued with the ◇ Q, as good as anything. South won and led a club to dummy's 10. When that held, a heart was ruffed and another club led to the jack and queen. Another heart was ruffed and the ♣ A was cashed. Declarer thus made one heart, five diamonds and three clubs for +110 and a great score.

TIP 18

When faced with a decision whether or not to compete higher, the player short in the enemy suit should leave the decision to the player who holds length in the enemy suit and should not take action in the direct seat.

(A)   Suppose the bidding has been:

Dealer North:	WEST	NORTH	EAST	SOUTH
Nil vulnerable		1♡	2◇	3♡(1)
	Dble (2)	4♡	4♠	?

(1)   Pre-emptive, 8 losers but below 10 HCP
(2)   For takeout

What action should South take with:

♠ 2
♡ A Q 9 7
◇ J 10 5 3 2
♣ 10 8 5

(B)   Suppose the bidding has been:

Dealer South:	WEST	NORTH	EAST	SOUTH
North-South vulnerable				1♠
	2♡	2♠	3♡	3♠
	4♡	No	No	4♠
	?			

What action should West take with:
♠ —
♡ A Q J 9 7 4 3
◇ K 8 4
♣ 7 6 2

(A)   The complete deal:

```
                    ♠ A K Q 5
                    ♡ J 8 4 3 2
                    ◇ 9
                    ♣ Q 7 4
     ♠ 10 9 8 6          N          ♠ J 7 4 3
     ♡ K 6 5                        ♡ 10
     ◇ Q          W         E       ◇ A K 8 7 6 4
     ♣ A K 9 3 2        S           ♣ J 6
                    ♠ 2
                    ♡ A Q 9 7
                    ◇ J 10 5 3 2
                    ♣ 10 8 5
```

At the table, South breached Tip 18 by bidding 5 ♡. He should have passed and North would have been in little doubt about what to do with 4 ♠. South also broke another sound rule: once you have shown your values, leave the decision to partner.

4 ♠ is one off on top and declarer cannot escape two off in practice. When South bid 5 ♡, West lost no time in doubling. East led ◇ A and shifted to the ♡ 10. Declarer took the ace and continued with A, K, Q in spades (South feeling the lash, no doubt, as each extra top spade appeared) to discard two clubs. The next spade was ruffed followed by a diamond ruff and club exit. West won and played king and another heart. Three down.

(B) The complete deal:

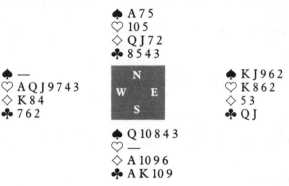

```
                    ♠ A 7 5
                    ♡ 10 5
                    ◇ Q J 7 2
                    ♣ 8 5 4 3
 ♠ —                                ♠ K J 9 6 2
 ♡ A Q J 9 7 4 3         N          ♡ K 8 6 2
 ◇ K 8 4            W         E      ◇ 5 3
 ♣ 7 6 2                 S          ♣ Q J
                    ♠ Q 10 8 4 3
                    ♡ —
                    ◇ A 10 9 6
                    ♣ A K 10 9
```

There is an illusion on hands like West's that because of the spade void, there is a sensational fit your way and therefore you can afford to push on. Bidding 5 ♡ ignores the fact that you have a partner.

In practice, West bid 5 ♡, passed to South who doubled. 5 ♡ was only one off but that was little comfort as 4 ♠ would be in deep trouble on repeated heart leads and should go at least two off. Again, had West passed the decision to partner, East would have had no trouble finding the right move.

Some partnerships have a sound principle in auctions such as these. When the player with the known shortage doubles in the direct seat, this says, 'I want to bid on unless you wish to pass.' That would have worked well in each of the above cases and when a player with marked shortage passes in the direct seat, it means 'I am happy to go along with whatever you wish to do, defend, bid on or double.'

TIP 19

Beware of passing out partner's takeout double with weak trumps or trying for penalties when you hold length in partner's suit(s).

(A) Suppose the bidding has been:

	WEST	NORTH	EAST	SOUTH
Dealer South:				No
North-South vulnerable	1♣	Double	No	?

What action would you take as South with:

♠ 64   ♡ J 5   ♢ J 8 4   ♣ 8 7 6 4 3 2

(B) Suppose the bidding has been:

	WEST	NORTH	EAST	SOUTH
Dealer North:		No	1♡	1♠
North-South vulnerable	1NT	2♠	3♢	3♠
	?			

What action would you take as West with:

♠ K Q 5   ♡ 9 6 4   ♢ A 9 2   ♣ J 10 8 4

Solutions: (A)   The fact that you have a tough problem does not mean you can shirk your duty. With a hand in the 0-5 point range, reply to a takeout double with a suit. With no 4-card suit, bid your cheapest 3-card suit.

The complete deal:

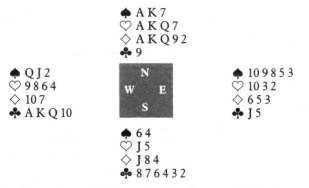

The hand arose in a world championship. At one table, South passed the double. North led a top spade and switched to hearts. Declarer was allowed to ruff the fourth heart with the jack of clubs, escaping for two down. North-South scored +300 but this was a woeful result. At other tables, South responded 1 ♢, as recommended, and some Norths bid 6 ♢ there and then. No doubt South awaited the appearance of dummy with some apprehension, but 6 ◇ proved an easy make. Although South holds only two jacks, what priceless gems they are.

(B)   The choices are No bid, Double, 3NT, 4 ◇, 4 ♡. Pass is timid as you are very strong for that 1NT response and partner's 3 ◇ showed extra strength. 4 ◇ is out of the question as you give preference to partner's first bid suit with equal length in each.

Many would be tempted to double but the length in each of partner's suits is a significant negative factor for the double. The choice between 4 ♡ and 3NT is close, but the shape of the West hand indicates no-trumps. In addition, West's spade values are likely to be far less valuable in 4 ♡ than in 3NT. The more high card strength you hold opposite shortage, the more the hand lends itself to no-trumps.

The winning decision is 3NT, as the full hand reveals:

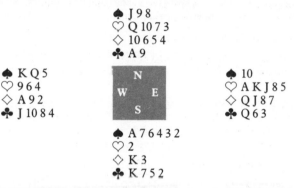

```
               ♠ J 9 8
               ♡ Q 10 7 3
               ◇ 10 6 5 4
               ♣ A 9
♠ K Q 5                        ♠ 10
♡ 9 6 4          N             ♡ A K J 8 5
◇ A 9 2       W     E          ◇ Q J 8 7
♣ J 10 8 4       S             ♣ Q 6 3
               ♠ A 7 6 4 3 2
               ♡ 2
               ◇ K 3
               ♣ K 7 5 2
```

3NT is not a great contract on the East-West cards, but it has the merit of being successful. The likely play is a spade to the ace, a spade back won by the king, heart to the jack, ◇ Q covered by the king and ace, ◇ 9, finessing and declarer has an easy 9 tricks. In 4 ♡, if the defence finds the club ruff early enough, the contract will be defeated.

Incidentally, West should have a serious talk to East about that 3 ◇ bid. The hand is way underweight. East's best action over 2 ♠ is a competitive double (*see* Tips 11 and 16), leading to a sound 3 ♡.

The hand arose in a USA national championship. At one table East-West supinely sold out to 2 ♠. At another, West doubled 3 ♠ after the above auction. A heart was led to the jack and East switched to the ♠ 10. This was attractive but it would take a diamond switch to defeat 3 ♠. South won ♠ A, played a club to the ace, ruffed a heart, cashed ♣ K and ruffed a club, ruffed a heart and ruffed the fourth club. The next heart was ruffed and overruffed but West was now endplayed and had to concede a trick to the ◇ K, giving North-South 730.

TIP 20

Prepare a comprehensive counter to the Unusual 2NT overcall or a Michaels Cue Bid by the opponents.

(A) The Unusual 2NT is part and parcel of the duplicate world and you need to be able to cope effectively with this interference. There are many possible schemes. This is one of the better ones.

Suppose the bidding has begun:

WEST	NORTH	EAST	SOUTH
1♡/1♠	2NT	?	

Double = Aiming for penalties. East is strong in at least one of the minors. If South bids a minor, West is requested to double if strong in that minor, otherwise to pass and give East a chance to double. Responder is sure to be short in opener's major.

3♣ = At least game-inviting with hearts.

If West opened 1♡, this shows heart support and at least 10 points. If West is minimum, West can sign off in 3♡. East can still bid on to game (or slam) with extra values.

If West opened 1♠, 3♣ shows at least a 5-card heart suit and may have spade support as well. Here, West can bid 3♡ with support and a minimum (East may still bid on), bid 3♠ without support for hearts but with extra spades bid 3NT or, with no clearcut continuation, 3♢.

3♢ = At least game-inviting with spades.

If West opened 1♠, this shows spade support and at least 10 points. West will sign off in 3♠ if minimum, but East can still push higher with extra values. With game values, West may bid 3♡ with four hearts in case East has four hearts as well as spade support.

If West opened 1♡, 3♢ shows 5+ spades and denies heart support (East would bid 3♣ with heart support). With a minimum, West may try to sign off in 3♠ with support or rebid 3♡ without spade support, but with extra hearts.

3♡ = Hearts, but weaker than the 3♣ response.
3♠ = Spades, but weaker than the 3♢ response.
3NT/4♡ or 4♠ = To play

Pass followed by Double of 3♣ or 3♢ later = Takeout. If you want penalties, double 2NT first.

4♣ or 4♢ = Splinter (singleton or void in the suit bid) with at least game-going values and support for opener's major. Opener is encouraged to look for slam with no wasted values in responder's short suit or with extra values. For example:

WEST	EAST	WEST	NORTH	EAST	SOUTH
♠ A Q 8 6 2	♠ K 9 7 5 3	1♠	2NT	4♢(1)	Dble
♡ A 8 6	♡ K 10 2	4NT(2)	No	5♡(3)	No
♢ 8 6 5 3	♢ 9	6♠	No	No	No
♣ K	♣ A 7 4 2	(1)	Splinter, short diamonds		
		(2)	Roman Key Card Blackwood		
		(3)	Two key cards, no trump queen		

(B)   Michaels Cue Bids are very popular, particularly over a major opening. Auctions such as 1♠ : (2♠) or 1♡ : (2♡) indicate the overcaller has 5+ cards in the other major plus at least 5 cards in one of the minors. What system do you have to cope with this intervention? Again, many methods exist. This is one of the better approaches.

Double = Looking for penalties. For example:

WEST	NORTH	EAST	SOUTH
1♠	2♠	Double . . .	

is equivalent to

WEST	NORTH	EAST	SOUTH
1♠	Double	Redouble . . .	

and East will hold the same sort of hand as for the redouble: short in opener's major, about 10 points or more and the ability to double at least two of the other suits for penalties. This is the best approach to catch them for penalties.

3-of-opener's major: Weakish raise, pre-emptive.

Other major: Asks for stopper for 3NT.

3♣ or 3♢: Natural, forcing.

3NT or 4-opener's-major: To play. 4-opener's-major is not a strong bid.

Pass and double later is for takeout. If you want to look for penalties, double at once.

4♣/4♢ or jump-other-major: Splinter, with support for opener's major, at least game values. Suggests slam if opener has little wasted in the splinter suit or has sufficient extra values.

2NT = Artificial, 10 points or more with support for opener's major. If enough for a game, it will not contain a shortage as responder would splinter with that. If opener is minimum, opener can sign off in 3-Major but responder will naturally bid on with extra values. If responder has a hand worth a natural 2NT bid, e.g. 10-12 HCP without support for opener and the outside suits covered, prefer to use the Double. For example:

WEST	EAST	WEST	NORTH	EAST	SOUTH
♠ A 6	♠ 8 7 4	1♡	2♡	4♡(1) . . .	
♡ K J 9 7 2	♡ A 8 5 4 3	(1) Same as 1♡:(No):4♡			
♦ A J 7	♦ 6				
♣ 9 8 7	♣ K Q 4 2				

WEST	EAST	WEST	NORTH	EAST	SOUTH
♠ A 6	♠ K 8 5	1♡	2♡	2NT(1)	No
♡ K J 9 7 2	♡ A 8 6 4	3♡(2)	No	4♡ . . .	
♦ A J 7	♦ K Q 8 6	(1) Heart support, 10+ points			
♣ 9 8 7	♣ 6 2	(2) Minimum opening			

PART 3: OPENING LEADS

In no other area of the play of the cards is there such a marked difference in strategy between the pairs game and either teams or rubber bridge as with the opening lead. At teams or rubber bridge, your objectives are pretty clearcut: declarer's task is to make the contract; overtricks are not even a secondary consideration; the task of the defence is to defeat the contract; conceding an overtrick to try to achieve that objective is of no consequence.

How differently do we approach the defence at pairs? It may be some time before we know what our par is: to defeat the contract *or* to hold declarer to the contract *or* to give away no more than a set number of overtricks. With our opening lead, we often have little idea which of these is our objective. Our only clue is the opposition bidding.

One thing is sure: we cannot afford to be generous, lighthearted or carefree with our opening lead. To give away a precious overtrick with our lead is an opportunity squandered. We may not be able to recover later in the defence. The best players at matchpoints are very, very frugal with their opening leads.

TIP 21

When you have a choice between a safe lead which is highly unlikely to defeat the contract and a speculative lead which may defeat the contract, stick with the safe lead. The speculative lead is far more likely to cost an overtrick.

At teams or rubber, the overtrick problem is immaterial. You can take whatever risk is necessary if you judge that is the best chance to defeat the contract. At pairs, you need to weigh the chance of defeating the contract against the risk of conceding an overtrick. If the risk of the overtrick is greater than 50%, and it usually is when the lead is unorthodox, you should stick with safety.

(A)   Suppose the bidding has been:

WEST	NORTH	EAST	SOUTH
			2♣(1)
No	3◇(2)	No	3NT
No	No	No	

(1)   Artificial, 23+ points (2) Natural, positive response

What should West lead from:

♠ J 10 9 6 5 4 2   ♡ Q 6   ◇ 8 4 3   ♣ 6

(B)

WEST	NORTH	EAST	SOUTH
		No	1NT(1)
No	3NT	All pass	

(1)   12-14

What should West lead from:

♠ J 8   ♡ 9 7   ◇ K Q 6 5 2   ♣ Q J 10 7

Solutions: (**A**)   The complete deal:

```
                    ♠ 7
                    ♡ J 9 4 3
                    ◇ K Q 7 6 2
                    ♣ K 8 5
♠ J 10 9 6 5 4 2                        ♠ 8 3
♡ Q 6                                    ♡ A 10 8 5 2
◇ 8 4 3                                  ◇ 10 5
♣ 6                                      ♣ J 10 9 7
                    ♠ A K Q
                    ♡ K 7
                    ◇ A J 9
                    ♣ A Q 4 3 2
```

The best chance to defeat 3NT is the ♡ Q. On some lucky day, you will strike partner with AJ10xx and the ♡ K in dummy or K-J-x-x-x and a miraculous entry. In a newspaper article, you will find this type of result where the ♡ Q lead produced spectacular success. Just remember that newspapers report news. You will not find a columnist recording the hundreds of occasions that such a lead cost a trick or cost the contract.

You should lead the safe jack of spades. There is no hope that the spade lead will defeat the contract. Partner can hardly have three spades so that even if the spades are set up, you have no entry to them. However, there is virtually no realistic hope of beating 3NT. The opposition bidding reveals almost enough for a slam. Make the safe spade lead.

On the actual deal, South has 11 top tricks. A heart lead gives South 12 tricks. Even worse, if East ducks the ♡ Q, South can squeeze East for 13 tricks. It is true that declarer can make 12 tricks also on a spade lead, but in real life no declarer is going to lead a heart to the king and risk making only 11 tricks, or even 10 tricks. On a spade lead, South is likely to run the diamonds and pitch the hearts, hoping for all 13 tricks.

(B)   The complete deal:

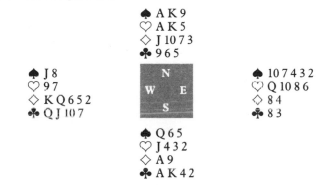

```
                    ♠ A K 9
                    ♡ A K 5
                    ♢ J 10 7 3
                    ♣ 9 6 5
    ♠ J 8                              ♠ 10 7 4 3 2
    ♡ 9 7              N               ♡ Q 10 8 6
    ♢ K Q 6 5 2    W       E           ♢ 8 4
    ♣ Q J 10 7         S               ♣ 8 3
                    ♠ Q 6 5
                    ♡ J 4 3 2
                    ♢ A 9
                    ♣ A K 4 2
```

The best chance to defeat the contract is a diamond lead. Some days East will have the ace. On other days, you may be able to set up four diamond tricks and East may have an entry and a diamond to get back to you.

Nevertheless, you should lead the queen of clubs. The chance of beating 3NT is low (North's failure to explore a major indicates length in the minors) and the chance of the diamond lead conceding an overtrick is high. The queen of clubs will not defeat the contract (barring miracles). You can hope for two club tricks, one diamond and a trick with partner. The strength of the club lead at pairs is that it is highly unlikely to cost a trick while the diamond lead may well give an overtrick.

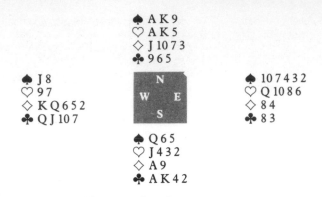

```
                    ♠ A K 9
                    ♡ A K 5
                    ◇ J 10 7 3
                    ♣ 9 6 5
  ♠ J 8                              ♠ 10 7 4 3 2
  ♡ 9 7          N                   ♡ Q 10 8 6
  ◇ K Q 6 5 2   W     E              ◇ 8 4
  ♣ Q J 10 7        S                ♣ 8 3
                    ♠ Q 6 5
                    ♡ J 4 3 2
                    ◇ A 9
                    ♣ A K 4 2
```

(Diagram repeated for convenience)

On the actual deal, on a club lead, declarer can score nine tricks via ♡A, ♡K and a third heart. On a diamond lead, declarer has nine tricks and can use the hearts to create a tenth. Holding 3NT to nine tricks will be a shared top.

If the diamond lead would have beaten the contract, do not waver in future. Accept the situation philosophically (and train partner to do the same!). You cannot expect to be right every time. What you need is faith that you are doing the right thing and that the conservative lead will give you the best result *most of the time*.

TIP 22

Against no-trumps, particularly 1NT or 2NT, be very reluctant to lead from a 4-card suit with only one honour. Even with two honours, 4-card suits present significant risk without great counterbalancing gain. To lead from 3 or 4 rags is usually safer than from a dangerous 4-card suit.

(A)   South opens 1NT (15-17) in third seat and all pass. What should West lead from:

♠ Q 9 8   ♡ Q 9 8   ◇ 8 7 5   ♣ K Q 9 5

(B)

WEST	NORTH	EAST	SOUTH
			1NT (15-17)
No	2NT	No	3NT
No	No	No	

What should West lead from:

♠ A 6   ♡ Q 9 4 3   ◇ J 8 7 6   ♣ 8 5 4

Solutions: (A)   You have no attractive lead and should choose a diamond. This is not likely to develop any tricks for your side, but is also least likely to give away a trick. The complete deal:

```
                  ♠ K 7 5 4
                  ♡ K 7
                  ◇ 9 6 4 2
                  ♣ J 8 4
  ♠ Q 9 8                        ♠ J 6 3 2
  ♡ Q 9 8            N           ♡ 10 6 4 3 2
  ◇ 8 7 5         W     E        ◇ A K
  ♣ K Q 9 5          S           ♣ 7 3
                  ♠ A 10
                  ♡ A J 5
                  ◇ Q J 10 3
                  ♣ A 10 6 2
```

In a pairs tournament, half the field led a club and declarer regularly made nine tricks for a shared top. Worst, of course, would be the ♣ K which allows South three club tricks if South picks to finesse the ♣ 8 subsequently. The rest led a diamond, won by East who switched to a major, usually hearts. Declarer has seven tricks and the play became a tussle over the eighth trick. Could the defence hold declarer to seven or could declarer garner the eighth? North-South +90 was a top for East-West. Even allowing declarer +120 was a reasonable score as there were so many 150s. One board proves nothing, of course, but this is a common enough situation and a passive approach will be best most of the time.

(B)   West has no attractive lead. With no long suit or no suit headed by a sequence, a passive approach is usually best. When the auction has been invitational, it is wise not to lead from a dangerous holding. Be conservative, accept the occasional loss and trust in the long term gains. The complete deal:

♠ Q J 4
♥ 8 7 5
♦ K 5 4 3
♣ K 10 3

♠ A 6
♥ Q 9 4 3
♦ J 8 7 6
♣ 8 5 4

♠ K 8 7 3
♥ 10 6 2
♦ 9 2
♣ A J 9 7

♠ 10 9 5 2
♥ A K J
♦ A Q 10
♣ Q 6 2

West should lead a club, which happens to defeat the contract. West grabs the ♠ A at first opportunity and leads a second club and the defence takes 2 spades and 3 clubs. That the club lead happens to work so well is a matter of luck. Defeating 3NT was not the purpose of the club lead. Your judgment should be that the club lead is least likely to cost a trick. If the club lead holds the contract to 9 tricks while other leads give declarer 10 then the lead has been a success.

A heart lead gives declarer a gift via the ♥ J. A diamond lead does the same, allowing declarer to score the ♦ 10 and 4 diamond tricks. These are not isolated cases. Leading from such moderate 4-card suits has a frequent mortality rate. Opening leads can be likened to playing the stockmarket: the speculative and risky can sometimes produce a windfall but most of the time, the outcome is a loss. A conservative approach will tend to produce better results (and greater wealth).

TIP 23

At pairs, ace leads against a small slam are more attractive than usual. Nevertheless, beware of leading an ace against 6NT (the ace will usually not run away) or leading an ace if the opponents have jumped to slam without bothering about Blackwood.

(A)
SOUTH	NORTH	
2♦ (1)	2NT (2)	(1) 2♦ = Game force, 23+ points
3♣ (3)	3♦	(2) 2NT = Natural, positive reply
3♠	3NT	(3) 3♣ = Stayman 3♦ = No major
6♠	No	

West to lead from: ♠ 8   ♡ 9 7 4   ♦ A 8 6 4 3 2   ♣ Q 10 8

(B)
SOUTH	NORTH	
1NT (1)	2♣ (2)	(1) 1NT = 12-14
2♦	3♠	(2) 2♣ = Stayman
4♠	4NT	
5♣	6NT	
No		

West to lead from: ♠ 5 4 3   ♡ J 10 9 6   ♦ 9 8   ♣ A J 7 6

Solutions: (A)   This deal from a pairs event gave declarer a top when the ♦ A was led. Any of the other 12 cards would have defeated the slam. The failure to use Blackwood should have been a clue. (Corollary: It may pay to use Blackwood even with a void if you intend bidding the slam regardless.) The complete deal:

```
                    ♠ 10 5
                    ♡ 8 3 2
                    ♦ K Q J 9
                    ♣ K 9 6 4
    ♠ 8                                 ♠ J 9 7 6
    ♡ 9 7 4             N               ♡ Q J 10
    ♦ A 8 6 4 3 2    W     E            ♦ 10 7 5
    ♣ Q 10 8            S               ♣ 7 3 2
                    ♠ A K Q 4 3 2
                    ♡ A K 6 5
                    ♦ —
                    ♣ A J 5
```

(B)   Lead the jack of hearts. Against 6NT there is usually no urgency to grab your ace unless the bidding has shown the existence of extremely long suits in their hands. It may however be vital to grab your ace early, as witness the complete deal:

```
                    ♠ A K Q 8 7
                    ♡ A Q 7 2
                    ◇ A 5
                    ♣ Q 8
   ♠ 5 4 3              N              ♠ 10 2
   ♡ J 10 9 6       W     E           ♡ 4 3
   ◇ 9 8                               ◇ J 10 7 6 2
   ♣ A J 7 6           S              ♣ 10 9 5 4
                    ♠ J 9 6
                    ♡ K 8 5
                    ◇ K Q 4 3
                    ♣ K 3 2
```

On the actual deal, leading the ♣ A would do no harm. However, the ♡ J lead preserves chances for defeating the contract. When declarer wins ♡ K and leads a low club, West must be alert to take the ♣ A. A quick count of the points around the table will be illuminating. West has 6 points, dummy has 21 and South has at least 12. East, therefore, has at most one jack and the ace of clubs is the only trick coming your way. You must make sure to take it. If West ducks the club at trick 2, declarer can cash the spade and diamond winners and score 13 tricks by squeezing West in hearts and clubs.

TIP 24

When you are strong in the suits outside trumps, lead a trump.

(A) South opens 3 ♣ at favourable vulnerability and all pass. What should West lead from:

♠ A J 8   ♡ Q 9 7 5   ◇ K Q 10   ♣ 7 6 4

(B) The bidding has been:

Dealer West: Both vulnerable	WEST	NORTH	EAST	SOUTH
	1 ◇	No	1 ♡	4 ♠
	No	No	Dble	All pass

What should West lead from:

♠ 8 3   ♡ Q J 2   ◇ A J 9 5 3   ♣ K J 9

(C) Dealer North: Nil vulnerable	WEST	NORTH	EAST	SOUTH
		4 ♡	No	No
	Dble*	No	4 ♠*	5 ♣
	Dble	No	No	No

*The double is used to show all round strength. Partner is expected to remove only with a good, long suit.

What should West lead from:

♠ 8 3   ♡ A K Q 10   ◇ A K 7 5 2   ♣ Q 7

Solutions: (A) The complete deal:

```
                  ♠ Q 7 5 4
                  ♡ K 8 6 3 2
                  ◇ A J
                  ♣ 8 5
   ♠ A J 8             N           ♠ K 10 6 2
   ♡ Q 9 7 5      W         E      ♡ A 10 4
   ◇ K Q 10                        ◇ 9 8 6 5 3
   ♣ 7 6 4             S           ♣ K
                  ♠ 9 3
                  ♡ J
                  ◇ 7 4 2
                  ♣ A Q J 10 9 3 2
```

The seemingly natural ◇ K lead allows 3 ♣ to make. After ◇ A and another diamond, declarer will ruff a diamond in dummy. Strong in each outside suit, West's best lead is a trump even though dummy has not shown any support. With three rags, a trump lead is most unlikely to cost a trick. Each of the other suits could be more damaging. After a trump lead, South cannot organise a diamond ruff and can be defeated by careful defence.

(B)   Strong in each outside suit, West's best lead is a trump, the 3 of spades. This was the complete deal:

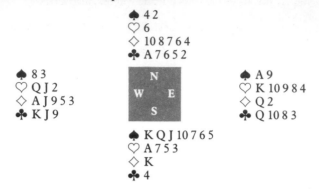

```
                    ♠ 4 2
                    ♡ 6
                    ◇ 10 8 7 6 4
                    ♣ A 7 6 5 2
    ♠ 8 3                             ♠ A 9
    ♡ Q J 2              N            ♡ K 10 9 8 4
    ◇ A J 9 5 3      W       E        ◇ Q 2
    ♣ K J 9              S            ♣ Q 10 8 3
                    ♠ K Q J 10 7 6 5
                    ♡ A 7 5 3
                    ◇ K
                    ♣ 4
```

As you have all other suits covered, the trump lead can minimise any ruffs in dummy and cut down on a possible cross-ruff. Second choice would be the ◇ A to take a look at dummy and then decide how the defence should go. After an early trump lead to the ace and a trump back, the defence would collect 500.

The hand arose in the Guardian Easter Tournament in London. West was the legendary Rixi Markus and East the equally legendary Zia Mahmood. 'I am ashamed to say,' wrote Rixi, 'that at the table I made the dreadful lead of the queen of hearts. Two heart ruffs in dummy gave the fortunate declarer 10 tricks.'

It is a comfort to us mere mortals that the superstars can also fall from grace from time to time. Full marks to Rixi who reported the deal against herself. Most top players are anxious to reveal only their good hands and their fragile egos will not admit to any imperfections.

(C)   It seems natural to lead the ♢K to take a look at dummy. If you tried that, your look would be shortlived. You are strong in two suits and East has revealed strength in spades. Following the same guide, a trump lead looks to be best. It certainly was on the actual deal:

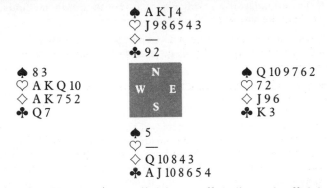

      ♠ A K J 4
      ♡ J 9 8 6 5 4 3
      ♢ —
      ♣ 9 2

♠ 8 3   ♠ Q 10 9 7 6 2
♡ A K Q 10   ♡ 7 2
♢ A K 7 5 2   ♢ J 9 6
♣ Q 7   ♣ K 3

      ♠ 5
      ♡ —
      ♢ Q 10 8 4 3
      ♣ A J 10 8 6 5 4

At the table, West led ♢ K, ruffed, heart ruffed, diamond ruffed, heart ruffed, then ace and another club. East cannot prevent declarer making 11 tricks. On an original trump lead, most unlikely to cost, the contract will go one or two down.

TIP 25

(a)   **If declarer uses a long suit trial bid and dummy rejects the invitation, be quick to lead that trial suit.**

(b)   **If the opponents use asking bids as part of their slam methods, prefer to lead the suit where the first ask is made.**

(c)   **If you have opened in one suit and partner was unable to respond, avoid bidding a second suit unless you want partner to lead that second suit.**

(d)   **Where the opposition bidding has started, 1-Minor : 1-Major, 3-Major, lead an unbid suit.**

(a)   The long suit trial is usually based on a suit where declarer is weak. It is common to have no more than one top honour in the trial suit. Suits such as A-x-x, K-x-x, x-x-x or x-x-x-x are the norm. If responder accepts the invitation, responder will have help in the trial suit, either an honour combination or a shortage to eliminate declarer's losers. If the trial bid is accepted, make your normal lead. There is no urgency to lead the trial suit.

If the trial bid is rejected and opener passes the reversion to 3-Major, be enthusiastic about leading the trial suit. If opener is weak and responder can offer little support, this suit is likely to be a promising source of tricks for the defence.

If the trial bid is rejected but opener bids game anyway, beware. Either opener had slam in mind or, more likely, the trial suit was a red herring on a holding like A-Q-x or K-J-10. Opener hopes this will tempt LHO to lead that suit.

(b)   The first asking bid en route to a slam is often made in the suit where the asker is weakest. It may be a suit of rags or a suit such as Q-J-x, a suit where the asker is anxious that there could be two losers off the top. Check the meaning of the reply to the ask. If the reply showed no control and the asker then signs off, you have all the evidence you need for the opening lead.

If the answer was negative but the asker bids the slam anyway, again be cautious. The asking bid may again have been chosen purely to tempt a favourable lead. Can't trust these opponents, can you?

(c)   Suppose the bidding has started:

WEST	NORTH	EAST	SOUTH
1 ◇	No	No	Dble
?			

It is not likely that East-West will win the auction. Unless West has a huge hand, West should be very discriminating in changing suit here. If West would like partner to lead a diamond, the best action is to pass. On the other hand, a rebid of 1♡, 1♠ or 2♣ by West would attract a lead of that suit. Such a change of suit when you are unlikely to end up as declarer is taken to warn partner off leading your first bid suit.

Therefore, change suit if you want the second suit led, but pass if you prefer partner to lead your original suit.

(d)	Dealer North:	WEST	NORTH	EAST	SOUTH
	North-South		1♣	No	1♠
	vulnerable	No	3♠	No	4♠
		No	No	No	

What should West lead from:

♠ 8 6 3   ♡ A 10 9 4   ◇ Q 7   ♣ J 7 3 2

Auctions that start 1♣ : 1♠, 3♠ or 1◇ : 1♡, 4♡ or similar are frequently based on 4-card support for opener plus a 5-card or longer minor. Whenever dummy has revealed a good, long suit and you are not strong in that suit, it pays you to lead an unbid suit. Declarer's strategy on such hands is to draw trumps and use the long suit for discards. Unless your tricks come quickly, you find that they often do not come at all. Even though an unbid suit may be a risky choice, you have to take the risk when dummy has revealed that long suit.

On the actual deal you needed to start with the ♡A or the ◇Q:

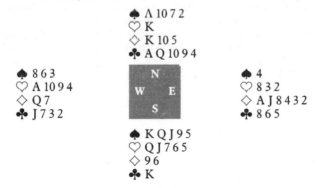

```
            ♠ A 10 7 2
            ♡ K
            ◇ K 10 5
            ♣ A Q 10 9 4
♠ 8 6 3          N          ♠ 4
♡ A 10 9 4   W     E        ♡ 8 3 2
◇ Q 7            S          ◇ A J 8 4 3 2
♣ J 7 3 2                   ♣ 8 6 5
            ♠ K Q J 9 5
            ♡ Q J 7 6 5
            ◇ 9 6
            ♣ K
```

When dummy has shown a long suit, it is no time for a passive lead such as a trump. On a spade or club lead, declarer will use the clubs to eliminate the diamond losers. You have to lead ◇Q (or ♡A and switch to ◇Q) to get what's yours.

TIP 26

When the opponents have bid well above their high card means, lean heavily towards leading a trump.

(A) Dealer North:
     Both vulnerable

	WEST	NORTH	EAST	SOUTH
		No	1♡	1♠
	2♡	4♣(1)	Dble	4♠
	Dble	No	No	Rdble
	No	No	No	

(1) Shows clubs plus support for spades

What should West lead from:

♠ 9 8 2   ♡ Q 8 5 2   ◇ A 9 7 6   ♣ K 6

(B) Dealer West:
     North-South
        vulnerable

	WEST	NORTH	EAST	SOUTH
	1◇	No	1NT	Dble (1)
	No	2◇	3♣	3♡
	4♣	No	No	4◇
	No	4♡	All pass	

(1) Takeout double of 1◇

What should West lead from:

♠ 9 7   ♡ A 5 3   ◇ A Q J 9 8   ♣ K 9 6

(A) They say that those of us who do not live beyond our means simply suffer from a lack of imagination. Bridge players who live beyond their high-card means are exercising their imagination in the play of the cards. Where will the tricks come from if not from high cards? From ruffs and more ruffs, that's where. How can you counter this strategy? By trump leads at every opportunity. Even if this sometimes seems to cost a trick in the trump suit, the trick usually comes back with interest by minimising the potential ruffs or crossruff.

The ♣ K may look badly placed but East's double of 4♣ shows high card values there, so that the ♣ K is not a wasted value. This was the complete deal:

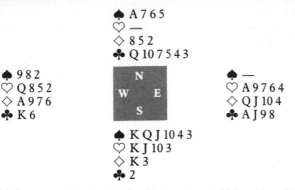

```
              ♠ A 7 6 5
              ♡ —
              ◇ 8 5 2
              ♣ Q 10 7 5 4 3
♠ 9 8 2            N            ♠ —
♡ Q 8 5 2                       ♡ A 9 7 6 4
◇ A 9 7 6     W       E         ◇ Q J 10 4
♣ K 6             S             ♣ A J 9 8
              ♠ K Q J 10 4 3
              ♡ K J 10 3
              ◇ K 3
              ♣ 2
```

The bidding marks North-South with less than half the points. Therefore lead a trump. A spade lead will ensure one down at least. Declarer can establish a heart trick, losing one heart to East in the process, but will then lose two diamonds and a club as well.

The actual lead was the ♡ 2, ruffed in dummy. A low club from dummy was won by East who switched to the ◇ Q: king–ace. West returned a diamond to East, but East was unable to lead a trump. Declarer was able to crossruff and make all the trumps separately.

(B)   Again the opponents have bid to a game when your side has at least 20 points. Heed the message and lead a trump on such auctions. This was the complete deal:

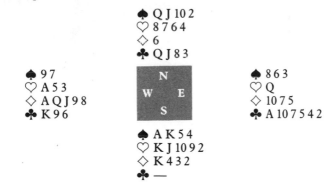

```
              ♠ Q J 10 2
              ♡ 8 7 6 4
              ◇ 6
              ♣ Q J 8 3
♠ 9 7             N            ♠ 8 6 3
♡ A 5 3                        ♡ Q
◇ A Q J 9 8   W       E        ◇ 10 7 5
♣ K 9 6           S            ♣ A 10 7 5 4 2
              ♠ A K 5 4
              ♡ K J 10 9 2
              ◇ K 4 3 2
              ♣ —
```

The actual lead, the ♣ 6, did not turn out to be a success. The queen was covered by the ace and ruffed. A diamond was led, but the trump shift was now too late. Declarer was able to ruff two diamonds in dummy. Declarer made an overtrick by ruffing two more clubs and dropping

West's king. The failure to lead a trump gave the contract. The club gave the overtrick.

From A-x-x, low is usually correct. Declarer will have to let West in with a diamond and then ace and another heart will stop declarer ruffing more than one diamond. The defence should then collect three diamonds and the ace of hearts.

Curiously, ace and another heart, which seems attractive on the auction, allows an expert declarer to succeed. South unblocks the ♡ 9 at trick 1 and wins the second heart in dummy. A club ruff, a spade to the 10, a club ruff and a spade to the jack is followed by a third club ruff. South then exits with the ◇ K to prevent East giving West a spade ruff. Declarer loses just one heart, one diamond and one club via a most elegant dummy reversal.

TIP 27

When declarer has bid two suits and you are strong in the non-trump suit, a trump lead will often work well.

When declarer bids two suits and dummy gives a preference to declarer's first suit, dummy often has more cards in the first suit than the second. If dummy gives preference to the second suit, dummy is bound to have greater length in that suit: with equal length, dummy would prefer the first suit bid. Declarer will often reduce the losers in the non-trump suit by ruffing them in dummy. If you have potential winners there, it pays you to lead trumps at every opportunity. This cuts down dummy's ruffing potential and gives you the best chance of scoring your winners in declarer's side suit.

WEST	EAST
♠ 5	♠ A 9 7 6 4
♡ 2	♡ Q 10 5 3
◇ A Q 10 9 6 3	◇ 2
♣ K Q 8 7 6	♣ A 4 3

WEST	EAST
1 ◇	1 ♠
2 ♣	2NT
3 ♣	5 ♣
No	

North leads the 10 of clubs. How should West plan the play?

You can scarcely afford to draw trumps. You are bound to lose one heart and it would be lucky to be able to play the diamonds for just one loser after trumps have been drawn.

On the auction, a heart lead was attractive. What can you deduce from the trump lead?

Corollary to TIP 27: Where a defender leads a trump after declarer has bid two suits, that defender is often strong in declarer's second suit.

On the basis that North is likely to be strong in diamonds because of the trump lead, a good plan is to win the lead with the king of clubs, cash the ace of diamonds and lead the queen of diamonds. You expect North to hold the king of diamonds.

Suppose North plays low on the queen of diamonds, do you ruff this or let the queen of diamonds run?

You should back your judgment and let the queen of diamonds run, discarding a spade from dummy.

The queen of diamonds holds the trick. On the next diamond, North plays the king. How do you plan the play from here?

On the actual deal, declarer won out after a tough tussle with the defence:

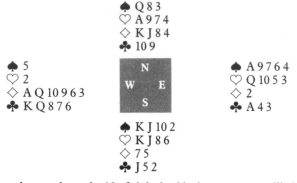

```
                    ♠ Q 8 3
                    ♡ A 9 7 4
                    ◇ K J 8 4
                    ♣ 10 9
    ♠ 5                              ♠ A 9 7 6 4
    ♡ 2                              ♡ Q 10 5 3
    ◇ A Q 10 9 6 3                   ◇ 2
    ♣ K Q 8 7 6                      ♣ A 4 3
                    ♠ K J 10 2
                    ♡ K J 8 6
                    ◇ 7 5
                    ♣ J 5 2
```

The good news about the 10 of clubs lead is that trumps are likely to break. Defenders rarely lead trumps when they divide 4-1. The bad news is that the diamonds are likely to lie badly.

After ♣ 10 won by the king, ◇ A cashed and ◇ Q led, if North had covered, declarer would have ruffed low, cashed the ♣ A and ♠ A and ruffed a spade, drawn the last trump and conceded a diamond to the jack. This loses just one heart and one diamond.

When North cunningly ducked the ◇ Q, declarer trusted his own analysis and let the ◇ Q run. On the next diamond, North continued his deceptive ways and followed with the king of diamonds, but declarer ruffed with the ace of clubs. Had he ruffed low, South would have overruffed. A second trump lead would then leave declarer with another diamond to lose as well as the heart.

Next came ace of spades, spade ruff, diamond ruff. South declined to overruff, but declarer was in control: spade ruff, queen of clubs and then diamond winners, allowing the defence to score just one heart and one club.

TIP 28

Be quick to double an enemy bid to focus partner's attention on that suit for lead purposes.

If the suit bid is artificial, the basic rule is that a double asks for that suit to be led. A double of a natural suit can also indicate the lead if the double would normally be interpreted as a penalty double. Most doubles of natural suit bids at a low level are takeout doubles of some kind or other.

Suppose you are playing in the 1988 Olympiad and you hear the following auction:

Dealer West:	WEST	NORTH	EAST	SOUTH
Nil vulnerable	No	2♦(1)	No	No
	3♣	No	3♠	No
	3NT	No	No	No

(1)   10-15 HCP, 6+ diamonds, no 4-card major

What should North lead from:

♠ K 4
♡ 10
♢ A Q J 7 5 3 2
♣ 9 8 3

If North had an ace as a sure outside entry, it would be best to lead the ♢ A and continue diamonds. The king of spades, however, is anything but a sure entry on the bidding so that starting with ace of diamonds and queen of diamonds may leave you with lots of winners but no entry. It is risky also to lead the queen of diamonds. If South has a singleton diamond, it may turn out that North scores no tricks at all.

With such a long suit, it is often a good idea to try to hit partner's entry so that partner can lead through declarer's guarded king. No doubt North had this in mind when she tried the heart lead in the Sweden vs Holland match in the 1988 Women's Olympiad.

The lead was no success, however, as the complete deal reveals:

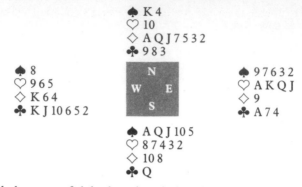

```
                    ♠ K 4
                    ♡ 10
                    ◇ A Q J 7 5 3 2
                    ♣ 9 8 3
  ♠ 8                                    ♠ 9 7 6 3 2
  ♡ 9 6 5              N                 ♡ A K Q J
  ◇ K 6 4          W       E             ◇ 9
  ♣ K J 10 6 5 2                         ♣ A 7 4
                       S
                    ♠ A Q J 10 5
                    ♡ 8 7 4 3 2
                    ◇ 10 8
                    ♣ Q
```

With the queen of clubs dropping, declarer had ten easy pieces.

The deal has unusual aspects. Why did East take no action over 2◇? A takeout double would be virtually automatic. Landing in 3NT was very risky, but at pairs one is prepared to run such risks.

The real culprit on the deal was the Swedish South who should have doubled 3♠ to show the strength there. Having failed to double 3♠, it was difficult for South to catch up by doubling 3NT later. Most pairs play that such a double of 3NT asks partner to lead the suit bid by the defence. That would be no use in this instance. South could double 3NT only if the defence had the explicit understanding that a double of 3NT here would ask for the first suit bid by dummy.

What was South thinking about when she failed to double 3♠? Not that the auction would end there or that the opponents might end in 4♠. That is far too fanciful. The likely truth is that South simply had a lapse of concentration, something one can ill afford at this game and especially not at pairs.

Without the double, it is impossible for North to hit on a spade lead. If South doubles 3♠ and East-West still play 3NT, the king of spades lead enables North-South to take the first twelve tricks. Of course, East-West are not likely to end in 3NT after 3♠ has been doubled, but what would you prefer? To have them play 3NT for 10 tricks (or 11 if North leads the ◇ Q) or to double 3♠ and end up defending 4♣ or 5♣? East-West might avoid 3NT, but some opponents may still end there (or even better, 3♠ doubled), some might land in 4♡ (a catastrophe after ◇ 10 lead and a second diamond), some may subside in 4♣, but many would land in 5♣ which can be defeated after a heart lead.

TIP 29

If you intend bidding at the 5-level or 6-level as a sacrifice or in a competitive auction when it is not clear which side can make what, make a lead-directing bid if partner is on lead and if the expected lead otherwise is unlikely to be the best for your side.

(A) Dealer East:	WEST	NORTH	EAST	SOUTH
North-South vulnerable			1♡	2♠(1)
	3♡	4♣	?	

(1) Weak jump overcall

What action should East now take with:

♠ J3   ♡ KQ98643   ◇ —   ♣ AQ76

(B) Dealer North:	WEST	NORTH	EAST	SOUTH
Nil vulnerable		No	1♡	2NT(1)
	4◇(2)	?		

(1) Weak, both minors
(2) Heart support, game-force, ◇A, no ♣A

What action should North now take with:

♠ KJ643   ♡ 53   ◇ 84   ♣ J542

Solutions: (A)   It is not clear whether they can make 4♠ or you can make 5♡. You should certainly bid on to 5♡, but consider what will happen if they push on to 5♠. Partner is likely to lead a heart and there is a far, far better lead for partner. You should bid 5◇ en route to 5♡ since you prefer the diamond lead. Partner should recognise that 5◇ is for the lead only and take you back to 5♡.

```
                    ♠ K875
                    ♡ 10
                    ◇ AKQ8
                    ♣ 10952
    ♠ 4                N              ♠ J3
    ♡ A752                            ♡ KQ98643
    ◇ J9764          W     E          ◇ —
    ♣ J83               S            ♣ AQ76
                    ♠ AQ10962
                    ♡ J
                    ◇ 10532
                    ♣ K4
```

5♡ is unbeatable, losing just one spade and one club. The best that North-South can do is sacrifice in 5♠. If East bids 5♡ and South bids 5♠, West may lead ♡A. Even if East discourages, it would be a mighty decision for West to shift to diamonds. On the normal club shift, South will make 5♠!

Even if East produces a spectacular suit preference signal with the king of hearts and West finds the diamond shift, 5♠ is only one down. How much easier to bid 5◇ now and double 5♠ later. On an immediate diamond lead, 5♠ doubled is two off: diamond ruff, heart to the ace, diamond ruff, ace of clubs. If they intend sacrificing, make them pay! +300 is not as good as 5♡ making, but is a lot better than letting 5♠ make.

(B) From your paltry values, it is highly likely that the opponents will bid to a slam. You could bid 5♣ but you do not really want a club lead. Partner has probably one defensive trick at most. A spade lead is the best chance for a second trick. That may not be clear to partner, but you can help. A sacrifice in 5♣ should not be too expensive, especially if they can make a slam. En route to 5♣, you should bid 4♠, running to 5♣ if they double you. The complete deal:

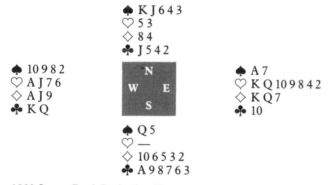

```
                    ♠ K J 6 4 3
                    ♡ 5 3
                    ◇ 8 4
                    ♣ J 5 4 2
 ♠ 10 9 8 2                          ♠ A 7
 ♡ A J 7 6            N              ♡ K Q 10 9 8 4 2
 ◇ A J 9         W         E         ◇ K Q 7
 ♣ K Q               S              ♣ 10
                    ♠ Q 5
                    ♡ —
                    ◇ 10 6 5 3 2
                    ♣ A 9 8 7 6 3
```

In the 1989 Staten Bank Invitation Tournament, Billy Eisenberg (USA) and Tony Forrester (Great Britain) both found the excellent 4♠ bid. Undaunted, both Easts continued with 4NT Blackwood and bid 6♡ after the reply. South led the queen of spades each time. One down. Note the effect of the lead of the ace of clubs or a diamond if South receives no helpful suggestion from North.

TIP 30

Have a clear understanding with your partner what is expected when you double a splinter bid.

The bidding has been:

Dealer West:	WEST	NORTH	EAST	SOUTH
East-West vulnerable	1♠	No	4◇(1)	No
	4NT	No	5◇(2)	No
	5♡(3)	No	5♠(4)	No
	No	No		

(1) Splinter: good spade support, values for game and a singleton or void in diamonds
(2) Shows one key card for spades, either the king of spades or an ace
(3) Asking for the queen of trumps
(4) Denies the queen of spades

What should North lead from:

♠ 7
♡ Q 7 3
◇ 10 8 7 6 4 3
♣ J 9 2

What would your answer be if South had doubled 4◇?

There are two schools of thought about how the double of a splinter should be used. One view is that it should show length and strength in the splinter suit and suggest a sacrifice, the other is that the double should be lead-directing.

Doubling to suggest a sacrifice is a reasonable approach, but the opportunities for its use will be rare. Sometimes the vulnerability will be wrong to sacrifice, on other occasions you will have defensive prospects and finally, you cannot yet be sure whether a sacrifice is indicated as you do not know how high the opponents plan to bid. You may be prepared to suggest a sacrifice against their game, but not if they push themselves to a slam. As partner cannot know this, partner may take a phantom sacrifice against their slam if you double the splinter, while you were happy to defend.

Doubling for a sacrifice has adherents because there is little value in doubling their splinter suit for the lead of that suit. As dummy will have a singleton or void in that suit, your side can score one trick at best. Even worse, if the double reveals that your side has strength in the short suit, this may persuade the opponents that they have few wasted values in this suit and may push them into a slam.

An ingenious idea suggested by George Rosenkranz of Mexico is to use the double of a splinter as lead-directing, but not of the splinter suit at all. The double asks for the lead of the suit *below* the splinter suit (excluding their trump suit, of course). In the auction on page 81, a double of 4 ◇ would ask for a club lead. Had their bidding been 1 ♡:4 ♣ (splinter), a double would ask for a spade lead. Had their bidding been 1 ♠:4 ♣ (splinter), a double would ask for a heart lead (as spades are excluded).

On the actual deal, the North-South pair were using this version of the splinter double and South passed 4 ◇. Working on the principle of 'the dog that didn't bark', North decided that South could have asked for a club lead by doubling 4 ◇. Therefore, South would appear to be more interested in a heart lead than a club. North thus led a heart. The complete deal was:

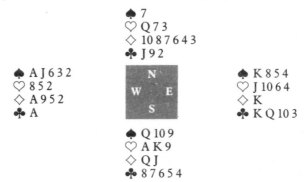

```
                    ♠ 7
                    ♡ Q 7 3
                    ◇ 10 8 7 6 4 3
                    ♣ J 9 2
   ♠ A J 6 3 2                        ♠ K 8 5 4
   ♡ 8 5 2          N                 ♡ J 10 6 4
   ◇ A 9 5 2      W   E               ◇ K
   ♣ A              S                 ♣ K Q 10 3
                    ♠ Q 10 9
                    ♡ A K 9
                    ◇ Q J
                    ♣ 8 7 6 5 4
```

East's splinter is not a textbook example, but the bridge world is full of players that do not pick up textbook hands. The defence speedily cashed three hearts and declarer later misguessed spades for two down.

At other tables, with less information, North often led a diamond. Declarer won this, played a club to the ace, a spade to the king and cashed the K-Q of clubs, discarding two hearts. When the jack fell, the 10 of clubs was led and the last heart discarded. When North was unable to ruff the ♣ 10, declarer had little difficulty in diagnosing the trump position, but twelve tricks were the limit.

As is so often the case, the opening lead is critical not just to defeat a contract but to hold declarer to the minimum tricks possible. The more lead-directing bids you have in your arsenal, the more often you will be able to give partner an indication of the best opening shot.

PART 4: DECLARER PLAY

The bidding is over, the lead appears, dummy comes down. This is the moment when good habits can bear fruit. Before you consider playing any card, stop and count dummy's points and your own. Then estimate whether you are in a poor contract, the normal contract or an excellent contract. This will have an important bearing on how you tackle the play.

In rubber bridge or teams, your task as declarer is straightforward. Your object is to make your contract, whether the contract is good, bad or indifferent. At pairs, the story is quite different. Suppose you find yourself in 3NT, but the sight of dummy tells you that you have missed the superior 4♡ game. If ten tricks appear comfortable in 4♡, you cannot be satisfied with making just 9 tricks in 3NT. That will leave you with a poor to bottom score. You must go all out to score the tenth trick in your 3NT, no matter how risky that may be. If 3NT making is a rotten score, 3NT one down will not be much worse. By risking the contract for the overtrick, you are risking only a little in order to gain a lot. Such thinking has no place at rubber or teams, but it is the heart and soul of pairs play.

You judge that your contract is normal. You now must consider their opening lead. Does it appear the usual lead? Was it made swiftly or was there much agonising before the choice was made? A quick lead means the same lead is likely at other tables. A slow choice means that other tables may fare better or worse. If the lead does not appear to be automatic and it gives you an extra trick, make sure you retain the edge received. If the lead is not automatic and looks very ominous, you will have to take chances to recover the ground lost.

If you feel your contract is superb, you should take no chances at all. In a doubled contract, making your contract will usually be enough to ensure an excellent score. Safety plays which involve conceding a trick to guard against a bad break usually cannot be afforded at pairs. In a doubled contract, however, be prepared to concede a trick if it makes your contract certain or more likely.

When you are doubled in a partscore and you are not vulnerable, your consideration is often not to make your contract but to hold the loss to just one down, −100. This may be a good score or it may salvage some matchpoints, whereas −300 on a partscore deal is bound to be a zero. If doubled in a partscore and vulnerable, you cannot afford even one down if the opponents cannot score a game. −200 is death in the partscore arena so that you will not do much worse if you are −500 or −800. You must go all out to make your contract.

TIP 31

Do not jeopardise a good score for the sake of an overtrick.

Overtricks are the life blood of pairs play. On occasion it may be
necessary to risk your contract for the sake of an overtrick. You need to
be able to judge the popularity of your contract. If you are in a poor spot,
you must do all you can to improve your score to match or better those in
the normal spot. If you are in the normal spot, you will do what you can
to try to eke out a trick more than the others.

However, if your judgment has landed you in a great spot or a gadget in
your system has allowed you to reach a magnificent contract which others
are unlikely to find, you must not give away the edge you have achieved
in the bidding. Simply making this marvellous contract is likely to be
enough to produce a good score. The overtrick, if achieved, is not likely
to gain much more.

Dealer East:		WEST	EAST
Both vulnerable		♠ K Q 9 6 4 3	♠ A J
		♡ Q J 3	♡ K 9 4 2
		◇ 10 8 3 2	◇ 9 7
		♣ —	♣ A K 5 3 2

WEST	NORTH	EAST	SOUTH
		1 ♣	No
1 ♠	2 ◇	Dble*	No
3 ♠	No	4 ♠	No
No	No		

*Competitive double, for takeout

How do you rate your contract of 4 ♠?

North leads ◇ K: 7-5-3, and continues with ◇ A South dropping the
queen. North continues with ◇6. You ruff with ♠ A and South follows
with . . . ♣ 2!

What do you make of that? How should you continue?

4 ♠ is an excellent contract and may not be reached at all tables. Making
4 ♠ will produce a very good score but one off will be a shared bottom.
Therefore, you must strive to make the contract and not concern yourself
with the possibility of an overtrick.

The best continuation is jack of spades, ace of clubs (pitching a
diamond), ruff a club and cash the king and queen of spades. If trumps
are 3-2, you are home and this line worked on the actual deal:

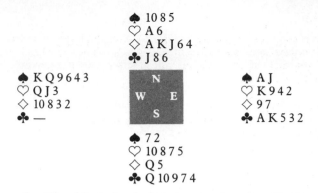

          ♠ 10 8 5
          ♡ A 6
          ◇ A K J 6 4
          ♣ J 8 6

♠ K Q 9 6 4 3   ♠ A J
♡ Q J 3   N   ♡ K 9 4 2
◇ 10 8 3 2   W   E   ◇ 9 7
♣ —   S   ♣ A K 5 3 2

          ♠ 7 2
          ♡ 10 8 7 5
          ◇ Q 5
          ♣ Q 10 9 7 4

In practice, West failed when he led a heart to the queen. North won and led a fourth diamond. This gave the defence a trump trick no matter what declarer did.

West tried to defend his play in the post mortem by claiming he was after an overtrick. What he was hoping for was that the ♡Q might hold the trick. He would then ruff his remaining diamond in dummy, discard the other hearts on the top clubs, ruff a club and cash the top spades. If the ♠ 10 dropped doubleton, he would then have 11 tricks.

There are several fallacies in this reasoning. On the bidding, the ace of hearts is highly likely to be with North and the actual defence was not hard to foresee. South's underruff is also a warning sign. It indicates South is trying to keep length with dummy's suit and therefore South will have started with a 2-4-2-5 pattern. The ♠ 10 is therefore probably with North and will not fall doubleton.

Above all, the 4 ♠ contract is excellent and bidding and making 4 ♠ should produce a shared top. To risk a bottom for a slightly better top is quite the wrong strategy.

TIP 32

When it is clear that you are in an inferior spot which will score less than the normal spot, take a line of play which will not be taken in the normal contract but which will provide a better score if it proves successful.

The kind of play involved may be playing for the drop in a suit where the finesse is the usual play or taking a ruffing finesse when such a play is not available for those in no-trumps. For example:

♠ A Q 9 3	♠ K J 7 2
♡ 9 7	♡ A K 4
♢ A 7 3	♢ 10 8
♣ A K 10 3	♣ J 9 6 4

1NT : 3NT

On seeing dummy, you see to your dismay that partner has taken a strange view by not using Stayman. The field will play 4 ♠ and if the club finesse works, they will make 12 tricks. If not, then 11 tricks. You cannot match this if you take the club finesse, too. If it works, you make 11 tricks and if it fails, you have 10 tricks. In either case you lag behind those in the normal spot.

Your correct play at matchpoints is to play off the ace-king of clubs, hoping North has Q-x. If so, you will have 11 tricks and outscore those who make 11 tricks in spades. If the queen of clubs does drop, that is not all good news: it means that you will have a top score, but partner may be slower in mending his bidding ways.

(A)

	WEST	EAST	Dealer East: Both vulnerable

	WEST	EAST	
♠	A Q 9 8 6 2	K 7 4 3	
♡	A 2	7 6	
♢	9	A Q J 10 8	
♣	A Q J 5	10 4	

WEST	NORTH	EAST	SOUTH
		No	No
1♠	No	3♢(1)	No
6♣	No	No	No

(1) Maximum pass, spade support and strong diamonds.

Opening lead: Queen of diamonds. North leads the jack of hearts. How do you rate the contract? Plan the play.

(B)

WEST	EAST	Dealer West: North-South vulnerable
♠ A K 4	♠ Q 5	
♡ A 8 3	♡ K Q 10 9 6 4	
◇ A Q J 3	◇ 7 2	
♣ K 8 3	♣ A 6 2	

WEST	NORTH	EAST	SOUTH
2NT	No	3◇(1)	No
3♡	No	4NT	No
5♣(2)	No	5NT	No
6♡(3)	No	No	No

(1) Transfer to hearts
(2) 0 or 3 key cards for hearts
(3) 2 kings outside hearts

The opening lead is the jack of clubs. How do you rate the contract? Plan the play.

Solutions: (A)   Your contract is excellent. Not every pair has that neat 3◇ bid available. With only 27 HCP, some pairs will miss the slam. You do not need to do anything extraordinary. Win the ace of hearts, draw trumps and continue with ace of diamonds and queen of diamonds. If South covers, ruff and then return to dummy with a trump to take one heart and two club discards on the diamonds. You can then try the club finesse for the overtrick.

If South follows low on the ◇ Q, discard your heart. North may win the king of diamonds, but you are home. Your club losers will disappear on dummy's diamond winners.

If you find that some Ramboesque declarer is in 6NT and makes it by taking the diamond finesse and the club finesse, do not begrudge him his victory. He may have won this skirmish but with that kind of strategy, he is not likely to win the battle.

(B)   You are in a dreadful spot. Your partner has obviously learned all the gadgets (such as transfers and Roman Key Card Blackwood), but it is high time he learnt something about basic pairs strategy. You should be in 6NT, of course, together with almost every other pair in the field. With 31-32 HCP plus a likely running suit, you should try for the no-trumps slam.

No point worrying about that now. You have to make the best of it. What will happen in 6NT? They are 12 top tricks (you play the ♡ K first, of course, just in case they do break 4-0) and those in 6NT will try the diamond finesse for the 13th trick.

Your only hope is that the diamond finesse fails.

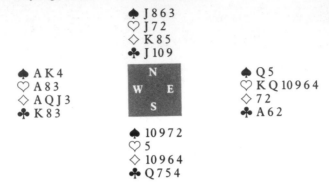

♠ J 8 6 3
♥ J 7 2
♦ K 8 5
♣ J 10 9

♠ A K 4
♥ A 8 3
♦ A Q J 3
♣ K 8 3

♠ Q 5
♥ K Q 10 9 6 4
♦ 7 2
♣ A 6 2

♠ 10 9 7 2
♥ 5
♦ 10 9 6 4
♣ Q 7 5 4

If the diamond finesse works, those in 6NT will make 13 tricks and you cannot beat them. If the diamond finesse loses, those in 6NT make 12 tricks and you still cannot beat them if you take the normal finesse. You should win the ace of clubs, draw trumps, cash your spades to discard a diamond and continue with ◇ A, then ◇ Q. If South has the king, you make 12 tricks while those in 6NT make 13, but that is immaterial. You could never beat them.

However, if North has the king, you will make 13 tricks while those in 6NT make only 12. The trouble with that top result is that partner may never learn to bid properly.

TIP 33

Assume the defenders are not doing you any favours. When dummy has an honour, a defender sitting over dummy should beware of leading that suit if holding a higher honour. Therefore, when a defender over dummy does lead that suit, it pays to play for the relevant honour to be with the other defender.

A novice may hand you a gift from time to time. A good defender will not. Where a defender makes a switch which could be handing you an extra trick, it is pounds to peanuts that the card that 'could be right' will be wrong. If you have a sensible alternative play for the same extra trick, it will usually pay to take the alternative.

There are many such situations and defenders tend not to lead away from honours where a significant risk exists (*see* TIP 42).

(A)
WEST	EAST	Dealer East. Both vulnerable			
♠ Q J 6 4 2	♠ A K 7 3	WEST	NORTH	EAST	SOUTH
♡ K 8 3	♡ 9 4			1♣	No
◇ A 7 6	◇ Q 5	1♠	No	2♠	No
♣ Q 7	♣ A J 10 4 2	4♠	No	No	No

North leads the queen of hearts. South takes the ace and switches to the 2 of diamonds. Plan the play.

(B)
NORTH	Dealer South: East-West vulnerable			
♠ K 7 6 2	WEST	NORTH	EAST	SOUTH
♡ J 6 5				1♣
◇ K J 8 7	No	1♠	Dble	1NT
♣ Q 5	No	No	No	

North-South play 5-card majors and 15-17 1NT opening.

SOUTH	
♠ A Q 3	West leads the ◇ 3 : 7-10-ace. South returns ◇ 6 : 4-8-Q. East cashes A-K-Q of hearts, West discarding ♠ 4 on the third heart. East switches to the 2 of clubs at trick 6. How should South play?
♡ 10 7 3 2	
◇ A 6 2	
♣ A 6 4	

Solutions: (A)   Do not expect South to have the ◇ K. If you duck, North will win the ◇ K and you will make 10 tricks if the club finesse loses or 11 tricks if North has the ♣ K. By taking the ◇ A, you may make 12 tricks. Draw trumps and tackle the clubs. If North started with K-x-x in clubs, you obtain two discards from dummy and both your diamond losers can be discarded. If North has the ♣ K but the clubs are not 3-3, you still make 11 tricks. (You may yet make 12 tricks if North has the ◇ K and K-x-x-x or longer in clubs, as North can then be squeezed). If South has the ♣ K, you make only 10 tricks.

If it turns out that South did have the ♢ K and has K-x-x in clubs, you will make only 10 tricks when you could have made 11 had you ducked the diamond. Still, you took the percentage position. Accept the loss and congratulate South . . . through gritted teeth, no doubt.

(B)   On the bidding, East is very likely to hold the king of clubs. South has 14 HCP, North has 10 HCP, the opponents hold 16. East has doubled and without the king of clubs, East would have a very ordinary double.

However, would East switch to a club away from the king with the queen in dummy? Not likely. Certainly not when there are several safe exits. It would cost East nothing to play the fourth heart and give you your ten. A sound defensive principle is to give declarer what declarer has anyway.

You could duck the club but a better plan is to rise with the ace of clubs, discard one club on the diamonds and play for the spades to be 3-3 or, less likely, West to hold four spades and the king of clubs, in which case the fourth diamond and 10 of hearts will squeeze West. The complete hand:

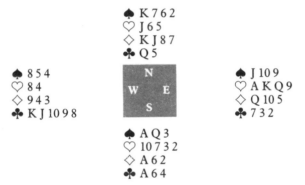

```
                    ♠ K 7 6 2
                    ♡ J 6 5
                    ♢ K J 8 7
                    ♣ Q 5
    ♠ 8 5 4                              ♠ J 10 9
    ♡ 8 4          N                     ♡ A K Q 9
    ♢ 9 4 3     W     E                  ♢ Q 10 5
    ♣ K J 10 9 8       S                 ♣ 7 3 2
                    ♠ A Q 3
                    ♡ 10 7 3 2
                    ♢ A 6 2
                    ♣ A 6 4
```

East's double is no thing of beauty, but that is not your problem. The good news is East is not your partner.

East's club switch was well-judged. Giving declarer the option to duck this to the queen was the only chance for the defenders to score another trick. If declarer rises with the ace of clubs, the result is nine tricks and a very good score (not a top as some pairs bid and made game), while making just eight tricks was below average. A sound principle at the table (and for life) is to trust others to be motivated by self-interest.

TIP 34

Where one opponent is known to have significant length in one suit, play that opponent to be short in another critical suit.

Often you have a suit which can be played equally well by leading from dummy first or from your own hand first. Deciding which hand is likely to be short may guide you to playing the suit to best advantage.

(A)

WEST	EAST	Dealer North: Nil vulnerable			
♠ A 5 4	♠ K 9 8 3	WEST	NORTH	EAST	SOUTH
♡ K 9 4	♡ A 3	No	1♢(1)	No	
♢ K 8 7	♢ Q 9 5 4 3	3NT	No	No	No
♣ K 10 9 5	♣ A 2				

North leads the 6 of hearts (fourth highest): 3-J-4. South returns the 8 of hearts: 9-5-ace. How should West plan the play?

(B)

WEST	EAST	Dealer North: East-West vulnerable			
♠ A	♠ K J 10	WEST	NORTH	EAST	SOUTH
♡ A 7	♡ 8 6 2		No	1♢(1)	No
♢ A Q 10 9 5 4 2	♢ K 3	2NT(2)	No	3♣	No
♣ K 4 2	♣ A J 9 6 5	4NT	No	5♢	No
		5NT	No	6♡	No
		7♢	7♠	No	No
		7NT	No	No	No

(1) Precision System, 2+ diamonds
(2) Game force, artificial enquiry

North leads the ♢ J. Diamonds are 2-2. Plan the play.

Solutions:

(A)

```
                      ♠ Q 7 6 2
                      ♡ Q 10 7 6 5
                      ♢ A
                      ♣ 8 7 4

  ♠ A 5 4              N              ♠ K 9 8 3
  ♡ K 9 4          W     E            ♡ A 3
  ♢ K 8 7             S               ♢ Q 9 5 4 3
  ♣ K 10 9 5                          ♣ A 2

                      ♠ J 10
                      ♡ J 8 2
                      ♢ J 10 6 2
                      ♣ Q J 6 3
```

In an American National, the popular play at trick 3 was to lead a diamond to the king. This was motivated no doubt by the desire not to open either of the black suits.

On the play so far, North has shown five hearts at least and South has at most three. As North has length in hearts, North is likely to have the shortage in diamonds. You could lead a diamond to the king or come to hand and lead a diamond to the queen. As North is likely to be shorter in diamonds, it is worth playing a spade to your ace to lead a diamond towards the queen. If North has doubleton ace, you have saved a trick. In the actual case, finding North with ace singleton also saves a trick and allows you to make the contract.

(B)   North's sacrifice in 7 ♠ suggests six spades (possibly seven, although then North may well have bid earlier). As North has the spade length, North is likely to be shorter in clubs. Therefore, the club finesse is likely to fail. The complete deal:

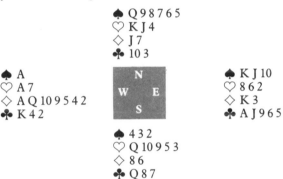

```
                    ♠ Q 9 8 7 6 5
                    ♡ K J 4
                    ◇ J 7
                    ♣ 10 3
   ♠ A                               ♠ K J 10
   ♡ A 7              N              ♡ 8 6 2
   ◇ A Q 10 9 5 4 2   W   E          ◇ K 3
   ♣ K 4 2              S            ♣ A J 9 6 5
                    ♠ 4 3 2
                    ♡ Q 10 9 5 3
                    ◇ 8 6
                    ♣ Q 8 7
```

World champion Gabriel Chagas declined the club finesse and played off six rounds of diamonds, the ace of spades and then the last diamond. This was the ending:

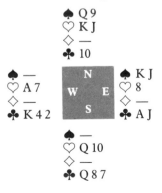

```
        ♠ Q 9
        ♡ K J
        ◇ —
        ♣ 10
  ♠ —            N        ♠ K J
  ♡ A 7     W        E    ♡ 8
  ◇ —            S        ◇ —
  ♣ K 4 2              ♣ A J
        ♠ —
        ♡ Q 10
        ◇ —
        ♣ Q 8 7
```

Chagas continued with the king and ace of clubs, forcing North to let the ♡ J go. Then the king of spades squeezed South in clubs and hearts and the grand slam was made.

Note the effect of North's attempted save in 7 ♠. Had he left 7 ◇ alone, declarer would have probably failed by taking the normal best chance of the club finesse. The clue of spade length with North gave West sufficient aversion to the club finesse to find the winning line.

TIP 35

With 5 cards missing, the most common break is 3-2. With 6 missing, the common break is 4-2. If desperate for a top, play for the maximum tricks, but normally play for the most common break.

WEST	EAST
♠ A K 7 3	♠ 9 4
♡ A K 4	♡ 8 7 2
◇ A 7 6 2	◇ 9 5 3
♣ 6 5	♣ A K Q 4 2

West is in 3NT on a heart lead. At rubber or at teams, West should duck a club at trick 2. At pairs, this is also the best play as the common break is 4-2. Play for a 3-3 break only in desperation.

WEST	EAST
♠ A K 7 3	♠ 9 4
♡ A K 4	♡ 7 2
◇ Q J 6 2	◇ 9 5 3
♣ 6 5	♣ A K Q 4 3 2

West is in 3NT on a heart lead. At rubber or at teams, West ducks a club at trick 2. At pairs, play for the common split and cash the clubs from the top. About 2/3 of the time, you make 10 tricks. On a 4-1 break, about 1/4 of the time, you are one off when ducking a club would have made the hand. Too bad. At pairs, frequency matters, not safety. You cannot afford to make just nine tricks and trail the field 2/3 of the time.

WEST	EAST
♠ A K 7 3	♠ 9 4
♡ A K 4	♡ 7 3 2
◇ A 6 2	◇ 9 5 3
♣ 7 6 5	♣ A K Q 3 2

How should West play 3NT at pairs on a heart lead? As above, you play for the common 3-2 break, but it costs nothing to take a slight precaution. Win the heart, play a club to the ace but return to hand with a spade before leading the second club. If North follows, play the king, queen, etc. However, if North shows out, you can now duck and deal with that 4-1 break.

WEST	EAST
♠ Q 10 9 6 3	♠ 8 7 5 4 2
♡ 8 5	♡ A K 3
◇ A K 7 5 3	◇ 9 2
♣ A	♣ Q 10 5

West is in 4♠ on the ♡Q lead. Plan the play. At rubber, you win and crossruff the hand. At worst you lose three trump tricks. At pairs, you should lead a trump at trick 2. On the normal 2-1 break, you will make 11 tricks. If it turns out that North began with A-K-J in spades and the diamonds are 5-1, you will go down. Tough luck. You cannot afford to score only 10 tricks if someone ruffs in with the singleton jack of spades when trumps are 2-1.

WEST	EAST
♠ A 8 4	♠ K 7 3
♡ A K 5	♡ J 6 2
♢ 5 4	♢ K Q J 3 2
♣ A J 4 3 2	♣ 10 5

West opens 1 ♣ and rebids 2NT over East's 1 ♢ response. East raises to 3NT. North leads the ♡ 10 and dummy's jack holds the trick. How should declarer continue?

Solution: West should play to set up the diamonds, but which approach is best?

Worst would be to lead an honour from dummy. This could lose to a singleton ace with North. To make four diamond tricks, the best sequence is heart to the ace and diamond to the king. If this holds, come back to the ace of spades and lead a diamond to the queen. You have four diamond tricks and ten tricks in all if the diamonds are 3-3 or North has ace-doubleton. In addition, your contract is secure if North has ace-singleton.

At rubber or teams you would adopt a different line. The above sequence fails if diamonds are 4-2 and South has A-x or either opponent has A-x-x-x. The secure line for nine tricks on any 4-2 break is a low diamond from dummy at trick 2 (this also caters for a singleton ace in either hand). Win any return in hand and lead a diamond to the king. Continue diamonds and you have three diamond tricks to go with your six top winners.

There is little to choose between the two lines at pairs. The 3-3 break is about 36% and North having A-x in diamonds is about 8%. In addition, leading a diamond from hand makes 9 tricks when North has ace singleton. The 'secure' line for nine tricks will bring in exactly nine tricks in 3NT almost 90% of the time: 36% for any 3-3 break, 48% for any 4-2 break, plus about 4% for singleton ace with either opponent. The rest of the time (5-1 and 6-0 breaks), both lines fail.

Thus, the lines break even 2% of the time (singleton ace with North) and each gains about 44% of the time. At teams or rubber, there is no contest between the two lines. At pairs, since the lines are effectively equal, go for the line that brings in the greater score. Play for 10 tricks.

TIP 36

When deciding whether to try for a quick discard to gain an extra trick, if you hold 6 cards or fewer between you and dummy, three rounds of the suit will usually survive. If you have 7 cards between you and dummy, two rounds of the suit are usually safe, but the third round will normally be ruffed.

(A)

WEST	EAST		Dealer East: Both vulnerable			
♠ A K 9 8 7 6	♠ Q 10		WEST	NORTH	EAST	SOUTH
♡ Q 3	♡ 7 5 4 2				No	No
◇ 5	◇ A J 9 6 2		1♠	No	2◇	No
♣ A 9 7 3	♣ K 6		2♠	No	4♠	All pass

North leads the jack of hearts. South cashes the king and ace and West ruffs the third heart with the ♠ 6. How should West continue?

(B)

WEST	EAST		Dealer North: Both vulnerable			
♠ K J 5 4 2	♠ Q 7 3		WEST	NORTH	EAST	SOUTH
♡ K Q 6 2	♡ A 9			No	1♣	No
◇ A 3 2	◇ 6 4		1♠	No	2♣	No
♣ 3	♣ A K 7 6 4 2		2♡	No	2♠	No
			4♠	No	No	No

North leads the ◇7 to South's queen. Plan West's play.

Solutions: (A) At teams or rubber bridge, you would play safe for ten tricks. Play a club to the king, a club to the ace and ruff the third club with the queen of spades. Then ◇A, ruff a diamond high, ruff your last club with the ♠ 10 and lose at most two hearts and the jack of spades.

As your contract appears normal, you should play for 11 tricks, hoping for the normal 4-3 split in clubs. With 7 cards missing, three rounds of a suit will usually survive.

```
              ♠ J 5
              ♡ J 10 9 6
              ◇ K 10 7 3
              ♣ Q 8 4

♠ A K 9 8 7 6       N         ♠ Q 10
♡ Q 3          W         E    ♡ 7 5 4 2
◇ 5                 S         ◇ A J 9 6 2
♣ A 9 7 3                     ♣ K 6

              ♠ 4 3 2
              ♡ A K 8
              ◇ Q 8 4
              ♣ J 10 5 2
```

Play ♣ K, ♣ A and ruff the third club low. Then ◇ A, ruff a diamond and ruff the last club. Ruff a diamond and cash the A-K of spades. If the jack of spades happens to drop doubleton you have your 11 tricks.

The risk of this line is if clubs are 5-2 and South has the doubleton and South can overruff the third club to lead a trump, thus eliminating the second club ruff. The total chance of that is below 10%. At teams or rubber, you need not take even that chance but at pairs, you should take that risk in order to try for the overtrick.

(B)   If you lead trumps at once, chances are you will make just ten tricks. It is risky to try to set up the clubs. You have seven clubs, they have six and you may run into an overruff if you tackle the clubs at once. There is no benefit in ducking the first diamond as you can reasonably escape for no diamond loser at all.

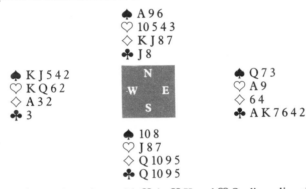

Win the ◇ A and continue with ♡ A, ♡ K and ♡ Q, discarding the diamond from dummy. Next ruff a diamond, followed by ♣ A and ruff a club. It would be too dangerous to play ♣ A, ♣ K and then ruff a club low. If you are overruffed and they play ♠ A and another spade, you will go off. The third round of clubs is not safe yet and if clubs are 3-3, you can benefit from this later.

After ruffing the second club, ruff your other diamond. Now try the king of clubs and discard your heart loser. If clubs are 3-3, you have some chance for twelve tricks. As it is, North ruffs the third club, but West still scores 11 tricks.

TIP 37

When you have two ways to try for an overtrick, take the line which offers the better chance of success without jeopardising the contract or a good matchpoint score.

(A)

WEST	EAST
♠ K Q 5 2	♠ A 4 3
♡ Q 10 8 4 2	♡ K 7 6
◇ 5	◇ A Q 6 4 3 2
♣ A J 3	♣ 4

Dealer North: Nil vulnerable

WEST	NORTH	EAST	SOUTH
	No	1◇	No
1♡	No	2◇	No
2♠ (1)	No	3♡	No
4♡	No	No	No

(1) Even though East has denied spades, West uses 2♠ to obtain more information in order to find the best contract. West's plan is to play 4♡ if East shows support and to play in 3NT otherwise.

North leads the 7 of clubs to South's queen. Plan the play.

(B)

WEST	EAST
♠ A K J 3	♠ 7 6 4
♡ K Q 9 4 3	♡ A 7 6 5 2
◇ A K J	◇ 8 7
♣ 8	♣ 9 3 2

North leads a club and West ruffs the second club. Declarer draws trumps in two rounds. How should West plan the play—
(1) If the contract is 6♡?
(2) If the contract is 4♡?

Solutions: (A) You should take your club ruffs before touching trumps, of course, so ruff a club, spade to the king and ruff your last club. You now lead the ♡ K, taken by South who plays another club which you ruff with the ♡ 8, as North follows. You cash the ♡ Q, but the ♡ J does not drop. When you play a third heart, South wins with the jack and exits with a spade. How do you play from here?

The main question is whether you take the diamond finesse or play for spades to be 3-3. This was the complete deal:

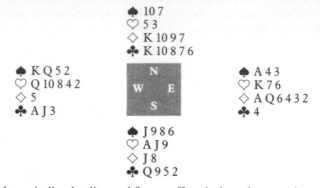

♠ 10 7
♡ 5 3
◇ K 10 9 7
♣ K 10 8 7 6

♠ K Q 5 2
♡ Q 10 8 4 2
◇ 5
♣ A J 3

♠ A 4 3
♡ K 7 6
◇ A Q 6 4 3 2
♣ 4

♠ J 9 8 6
♡ A J 9
◇ J 8
♣ Q 9 5 2

Mathematically, the diamond finesse offers the best chance and you should win ♣ Q and finesse the ◇ Q. When this comes off, you have a discard for your fourth spade and 11 tricks. The diamond finesse is 50% while the 3-3 spade break is less likely. Even if the diamond finesse loses you make 10 tricks as the ◇ A takes care of the fourth spade.

You could back your judgment of the spade position. If you trust their signalling and they have shown 3-3 in spades, you might prefer the spade play. If it turns out that North has four spades, play off your trumps. If North has the ◇ K as well, a show-up squeeze will develop.

It is risky to test the spades and if they are not 3-3, to fall back on the diamond finesse. If that also loses, you could go one down. Making 11 tricks will be a top board, making 10 will not be too bad, but going off will be a revolting score.

WEST   EAST
♠ A K J 3   ♠ 7 6 4
♡ K Q 9 4 3   ♡ A 7 6 5 2
◇ A K J   ◇ 8 7
♣ 8   ♣ 9 3 2

(Diagram repeated for convenience)

(B) (1) In 6♡, you should combine the spade and diamond chances. After drawing trumps, cash the ♠ A, ♠ K. If the ♠ Q has dropped, you are home. If not, cross to dummy and take the diamond finesse. If that works you can discard dummy's last spade and you are home.

The chance of North having Q-x in spades is only 8%, but in 6♡, that extra chance is worthwhile. 6♡ is a very good contract which very few tables will reach. Making 6♡ will give you a top board while going one down or two down will be almost the same bottom score. The extra undertrick is almost free and that justifies the additional chance of making the slam, improving your odds beyond the mere 50% of either the spade finesse or the diamond finesse.

(2)   4♡ will be the normal contract. This is perfectly safe for 11 tricks and you must not risk making just ten tricks. Cash the A-K of diamonds first. On a miracle day, the ♢ Q might fall and you have your 12 tricks. If not, cash the ♠ A (in case the ♠ Q is singleton), then ruff your ♢ J and take the spade finesse. You will make 12 tricks, a bit over 50%.

If you cash ♠ A-K first, you may add about 8% to your chances of making 12 tricks, but if the ♠ Q does not drop and you decide to take the diamond finesse, there is now almost a 40% chance of making only 10 tricks. (You may still make 11 tricks if the diamond finesse loses, but North is out of spades.) Making 10 tricks will be a bottom. The slight extra chance for the extra overtrick by cashing the ♠ A-K is not justified by the significant risk of scoring a zero.

TIP 38

Part A: When the defence does something quite strange, you must stop and ask yourself why. Do not play on until you have found a satisfactory answer. Assume that their play has an underlying logic and when you discover it, act accordingly.

Corollary: If you assume the opponents are morons, you will find yourself as the one with egg on your face.

Part B: When an opponent uses a pre-emptive or conventional bid to show significant length in one or two suits, make a mental note of the number of cards shown in the long suit(s). Then focus on the number of cards played by that defender in the short suits. The holding in the last short suit will often be revealed.

On the following problem, declarer did not bother to ask himself why East had defended as he did. Would you have done better?

NORTH	Dealer East: Nil vulnerable			
♠ K 8 6	WEST	NORTH	EAST	SOUTH
♡ A K J 3			2♠ (1)	No
◇ A 10 4 2	No	Dble	No	3♡
♣ A 9	No	4♡	All pass	
	(1) Weak, 6 spades, 6-10 HCP			

SOUTH

♠ J 5 3   West leads the 9 of spades, low, queen
♡ 9 8 7 2   from East and South drops the 5. At
◇ Q 7   trick 2 East switches to the 5 of
♣ K Q 7 5   diamonds. What do you make of that?

In any event, you play low from hand, West plays the jack and you take the ace. How should declarer continue?

Solution: It is strange that East did not cash the ♠ A and give West a spade ruff. The ♠ 9 is clearly a singleton or a doubleton, so what can East be thinking?

Suppose you held only two spades and that the lead were a doubleton. On the third spade you would in fact discard a diamond, but what if you had no diamond to discard? Now you might ruff and find that West was unable to overruff. If so, you would place the ♡ Q with East and thus avoid the losing heart finesse.

This was the complete deal:

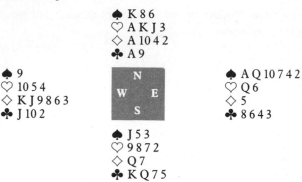

East was frightened that if South had a doubleton spade, ◇ K-x, ♣ K and ♡ 10-x-x-x, South would ruff the third spade with the ♡ 10 and now East would not score the ♡ Q. The switch to the ◇ 5 was ill-advised, but perhaps East knew his customer.

South played by the book instead of playing the player. He won West's ◇ J with the ace, cashed a top trump, came to hand with a club and took the heart finesse. East won, cashed ♠ A and gave West a spade ruff. West cashed the ◇ K for two down.

If South diagnoses East's reluctance to continue spades, South can make East pay dearly for this slip. Win the ◇ A and cash the ♡ A and ♡ K. When the queen drops, play a diamond to the queen and king without cashing the ♡ J. West will probably switch to a club. Win the ♣ A, cash the ◇ 10 on which one spade is discarded and ruff the last diamond.

As East has shown up with six spades (on the bidding) two hearts and only one diamond, East is the one with four clubs. Therefore, play a heart to the jack and then cash the last heart, discarding a spade from hand. On this, East will be squeezed in spades and clubs and declarer will score 11 tricks. That will teach East not to treat you so cavalierly in future.

TIP 39

Without a compelling reason, do not hold up an ace at a trump contract.

The hold-up with A-x or A-x-x at no-trumps is quite common when no other suit is as dangerous. Such a hold-up at trumps can be necessary, but the occasions are rare. Make sure you have a sound basis for the hold-up.

(A)

WEST	EAST	Dealer West: North-South
♠ A 2	♠ K 7 6 5 4 3	vulnerable
♡ 10 6 5 4	♡ 8 7 3	
◇ 9 8 3	◇ A 7 2	
♣ A K Q 7	♣ 4	

WEST	NORTH	EAST	SOUTH
1NT(1)	No	2♡(2)	No
2♠	No	No	No

(1) 12-14 (2) Transfer to spades

North leads the ◇ K. Plan the play.

(B)

WEST	EAST	Dealer South: Both vulnerable
♠ K	♠ A J 10 9	
♡ K 9 8 7 5	♡ A 6 4 3 2	
◇ A J 3	◇ 9 6	
♣ Q J 10 9	♣ 8 5	

WEST	NORTH	EAST	SOUTH
		No	No
1♡	No	3♡(1)	No
4♡	No	No	No

(1) Not wishing to punish partner for a light third-hand opening.

North leads the king of diamonds. Plan the play.

(C)

WEST	EAST	Dealer West: North-South
♠ A Q J 10 6 4	♠ K 9 2	vulnerable
♡ Q 9	♡ J 10	
◇ 7 5 4	◇ A 9 2	
♣ 3 2	♣ A Q 10 8 7	

WEST	NORTH	EAST	SOUTH
2♠(1)	No	2NT(2)	No
3♠(3)	No	4♣	All pass

(1) Weak two (2) Ogust enquiry
(3) Maximum plus two top trumps

North cashes the ♡ A-K and switches to the queen of diamonds. Plan West's play.

(D)

WEST	EAST '	Dealer East: Both vulnerable
♠ K J 10 9 2	♠ A 6 4 3	
♡ A 7 3	♡ 9 4 2	
◇ A J	◇ K 3	
♣ 6 4 2	♣ K Q J 8	

WEST	NORTH	EAST	SOUTH
		1♣	No
1♠	No	2♠	No
4♠	No	No	No

North leads the king of hearts. Plan the play.

Solutions: (A) Play your ace of diamonds at once. There is no benefit in letting the king of diamonds go and there is a significant risk. After ♢ A, cash ♠ A, ♠ K and run the clubs, discarding two red losers. If trumps are 3-2, you make nine tricks.

If you let the first diamond go, the opponents may switch to hearts. You might then lose one diamond, three hearts and a spade and make only eight tricks. It could be even worse if North has a singleton or a doubleton heart and only two spades. For example, if North has ♠ J10 ♡ KQ ♢ KQJ54 ♣ 9853 and finds the heart switch at trick two, South can overtake the second heart, cash the ♡ J and lead a fourth heart. Now a ruff by North will uppercut dummy and give the defence two trump tricks.

(B) Do not duck the king of diamonds. If you do, you are limited to ten tricks if the opponents take two clubs. If trumps are 2-1, you have a good show for 11 tricks. Win ♢ A, cash ♡ K, ♠ K and cross to ♡ A. Discard a diamond on the ♣ A and lead the ♠ J: if South has the ♠ Q, you will be able to discard your second diamond loser. If trumps are 3-0, it is vital to take the first diamond. Win ♢ A, cash ♡ K and if trumps are 3-0, lead ♠ K and overtake with the ♠ A. Then lead ♠ J. If South has the ♠ Q, you have a good chance to make your contract. There is a slight risk of going two down by this line, but if you do, you will have company. The strong declarers will play the same way.

(C) Do not hold off with the ♢ A. There is a chance for 11 tricks, but if you duck the diamond, you can make 10 tricks at best. Win ♢ A, play ♠ 2 to ♠ A and finesse the ♣ Q. If this holds, cash ♣ A and ruff a club. If North started with something like:

♠ xx   ♡ A K x x   ♢ Q J x x   ♣ K x x

you have set up two club winners. Draw trumps and discard the diamonds losers on the club winners.

(D) Here you should duck the first heart. The contract depends essentially on avoiding a trump loser. However, whether or not there is a loser in trumps, you may score an extra trick by letting the first heart go. Win the second heart and lead the ♠ J (maybe North will cover). If not, take ♠ A and ♠ K.

Then start on the clubs. If the clubs are 3-3 and the player with the ace of clubs started with two hearts, you can discard a heart loser on the thirteenth club, whether or not there is a trump loser. For example, suppose North started with:

♠ xx   ♡ K Q J x x   ♢ xxx   ♣ xxx

If you take the first heart, South will lead a heart on coming in with the ace of clubs. If you hold up the ♡ A and win the second heart, South has no hearts left. You now lose only one heart and one club. Here the hold-up was justified since it gave you a fair chance for an extra trick.

TIP 40

When a player takes action with significantly less in HCP than expected for that level of bidding, base your play on that player having extreme distribution.

If a player bids at a high level with full high card values, the shape may not be wild. If the high card values are not present, what justifies a player entering at such a high level? There must be distributional compensation. The lower the high card content, the more extreme the shape.

NORTH
- ♠ K 10 7
- ♡ 3
- ♢ Q J 9 3 2
- ♣ A J 10 4

SOUTH
- ♠ 8
- ♡ A K J 10 8 7 5
- ♢ 6
- ♣ K 6 5 3

Dealer South: Both vulnerable

WEST	NORTH	EAST	SOUTH
			4♡
Dble*	No	No	No

*The double is primarily for takeout but partner is allowed to pass with defensive values.

West leads the ♠ A : 7-2-8, and switches to ♢ 5 at trick 2 : Q-A. East returns the ♢ 7 and South ruffs.

What do you make of the play so far. Where are the missing cards likely to be? What shape do you expect West to have?

Plan the play.

Solution: East has turned up with the ace of diamonds, yet West doubled 4♡ for takeout. West led the ace of spades and appears to have the king of diamonds. What else? The queen of hearts is likely to be with East, partly because the double was for takeout and partly because East passed it when there is a 9-card spade fit for East-West. That leaves West with the queen of clubs and the lower spade honours. So . . . . .

♠ AQJ?   ♡ ?   ♢ K???   ♣ Q???.

Barely enough for a 1-level double, let alone a 4-level double, isn't it? Give the vulnerability, it is highly likely that West has a 5-4-4-0 pattern, void in hearts, of course. If you accept that, how should you continue?

The successful line is a low club to the jack which holds, followed by the ♡3 from dummy and finesse your 8. All of this is necessary as the complete deal looks like this:

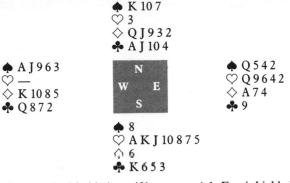

```
                    ♠ K 10 7
                    ♡ 3
                    ◇ Q J 9 3 2
                    ♣ A J 10 4
  ♠ A J 9 6 3                        ♠ Q 5 4 2
  ♡ —             N                  ♡ Q 9 6 4 2
  ◇ K 10 8 5    W   E                ◇ A 7 4
  ♣ Q 8 7 2       S                  ♣ 9
                    ♠ 8
                    ♡ A K J 10 8 7 5
                    ◇ 6
                    ♣ K 6 5 3
```

After a heart to the 8 holds (even if hearts are 4-1, East is highly likely to have Q-9-x-x to pass the double), South continues with ♡A, ♡K and ♡J. Later South draws East's last trump and repeats the club finesse to score ten tricks.

There are two traps: if you cash the king of clubs and then try to finesse, East ruffs the second club and you cannot pick up East's queen. One off. It seems natural to finesse the 10 or J of hearts on the first round, but this also leads to defeat with the actual break. Given West's aggressive double, you should play for the hearts 5-0.

In practice, declarer made the hand on the above line. After the hand East complained, 'Didn't you see my 2 of spades, asking for a club switch. If you play a club at trick 2, I can put you in with a diamond after I score the ♡Q and get the club ruff.' 'Not exactly,' retorted West, 'it has to be a club opening lead. If I switch to a club at trick 2, South can pitch the diamond loser on the king of spades and make 11 tricks!'

PART 5: DEFENCE

This area is an excellent one on which to concentrate. Players who can defend well have a significant edge. The standard of defence among most players is generally lower than other areas of the game. Most players can handle their constructive bidding competently and can play the dummy reasonably well. When it comes to defending, however, there are many who adopt a futile line or who slop trick after trick. It is no compliment for a defender to be known as 'The Magician'—one who makes tricks disappear.

At rubber bridge or teams, your task as a defender is clearcut. Defeat the contract. If it happens to cost an overtrick, too bad. You are prepared to squander an overtrick or two for even a remote chance of putting the contract down.

At matchpoints, defence is far, far tougher. Your object may not be to defeat the contract at all. You may achieve a good score if you can restrict declarer to, say ten tricks in 3NT instead of allowing eleven tricks. When dummy appears, you should estimate how successful declarer is likely to be. Count dummy's points, estimate declarer's points. Does declarer appear to have more than enough for the contract? If so, your main purpose will be to restrict the overtricks. Have they bid a game or a slam on relatively few points? Then you will need to go all out to defeat the contract. Try to judge the popularity of the contract. If few pairs are likely to bid this game or slam, it will hardly matter whether you concede an overtrick. If they make the game, they are headed for a good score. Defeating their contract then will be your objective.

Good defence is often a matter of partnership co-operation and strong partnerships play close attention to their signalling agreements. In defence you can do with all the help you can get.

One of the most important aspects in matchpoint defence is 'Take your tricks'. When it becomes clear that you cannot defeat their contract, try to ensure none of the tricks that you could take go begging.

TIP 41

Take the tricks that are yours unless they cannot disappear. In particular, if there is any danger that declarer might be able to discard the suit in which you have a winner, grab your winner.

It may not be essential to defeat the contract. It is vital to take all the tricks that belong to you. If you fail to take a trick that you could reasonably have taken, you are headed for a poor score.

(A)

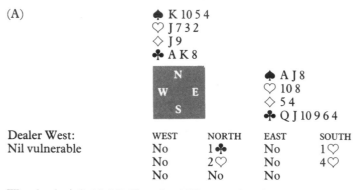

♠ K 10 5 4
♡ J 7 3 2
♢ J 9
♣ A K 8

♠ A J 8
♡ 10 8
♢ 5 4
♣ Q J 10 9 6 4

Dealer West:	WEST	NORTH	EAST	SOUTH
Nil vulnerable	No	1♣	No	1♡
	No	2♡	No	4♡
	No	No	No	

West leads ♠ 2: 10-J-3. How should East continue?

(B)

♠ K 8 6
♡ A K J 3
♢ A 10 4 2
♣ A 9

♠ A Q 10 7 4 2
♡ Q 6
♢ 5
♣ 8 6 4 3

Dealer East:	WEST	NORTH	EAST	SOUTH
Nil vulnerable			2♠ (1)	No
	No	Dble	No	3♡ (2)
	No	4♡	All pass	

(1)   Weak two
(2)   North-South use the Lebensohl Convention in this situation in which 2NT by South is used for all revolting hands. South's 3♡ is therefore constructive, about 7-10 points.

West leads the 9 of spades: 6-Q-5. How should East continue?

Solutions: (A)   Partner's lead of ♠2 indicates a 4-card suit, so that South has a second spade. It could be vital to cash ♠A at trick 2 and that is what you should do. At teams or at rubber you might switch to a diamond (or a club) but at matchpoints, ♠A must be taken, lest it disappear. Where could it go? Here is the complete deal:

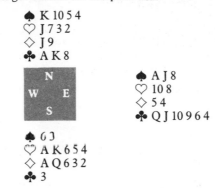

```
              ♠ K 10 5 4
              ♡ J 7 3 2
              ◇ J 9
              ♣ A K 8
♠ Q 9 7 2        N           ♠ A J 8
♡ Q 9                        ♡ 10 8
◇ K 10 8 7    W     E        ◇ 5 4
♣ 7 5 2          S           ♣ Q J 10 9 6 4
              ♠ 6 3
              ♡ A K 6 5 4
              ◇ A Q 6 3 2
              ♣ 3
```

If you cash the ace of spades, declarer makes just 10 tricks. That was worth a 75% score to East-West. If you switch, declarer can pitch the second spade on the clubs and score 11 tricks. That was worth only 15% to East-West.

Note that if East switches to the ◇5, declarer should follow TIP 33 (*see* page 89). As dummy has an honour, East is unlikely to lead that suit with the king. Therefore, South should reject the diamond finesse and grab the chance of the overtrick via the club discard.

(B)   Partner's lead of the 9 of spades could be a singleton or a doubleton. If it is a singleton, you need to take the ♠A and give partner the spade ruff. If it is a doubleton, it may still be vital to take your ♠A. Perhaps declarer can discard a spade from hand (with K-Q-x in diamonds, for example) or even two from dummy (with K-Q-J-x in clubs, perhaps).

There is a slight risk that if the spades are 2-2 and South has ♡10 and no useful discard on the third spade that you may miss out on ♡Q. That risk is not nearly as great as the possibility of losing ♠A (and perhaps a spade ruff).

Still, you need to know your customers . . . For what actually happened on this deal and what could have happened, *see* TIP 38.

TIP 42

When you sit over dummy with an honour card and dummy has the card below your honour, be very careful about switching to that suit. In general, be extremely reluctant to switch to such a suit, as it often gives declarer an extra trick.

At rubber bridge or teams, you may risk conceding an overtrick when switching to a suit if that suit offers the best chance of defeating the contract. At pairs, such a risk is usually not justified. Be very confident of your ground before you switch to any of the suits shown below.

(A)	Dummy	(B)	Dummy
	J 6 2		J 6 2
	EAST		EAST
	Q 9 3		K 9 5

If East switches to this suit, East runs the risk of finding any of these layouts:

(A1)   J 6 2   Declarer has two tricks. If East
    10 7 5 4   Q 9 3   leads the suit, East gives declarer a
         A K 8   chance to make three tricks.

(A2)   J 6 2   Declarer has one trick and cannot
    K 8 7 5   Q 9 3   score two tricks unless the defence
         A 10 4   starts the suit. If East leads the
             suit, South ducks and the
remaining A-10 tenace allows South to finesse against East's queen later.

(A3)   J 6 2   Declarer has one trick and cannot
    A 8 7 5   Q 9 3   legitimately score two tricks. If
         K 10 4   East leads the suit, South ducks
and whether West takes the ace or not, South can make two tricks by finessing the 10 later.

(B1)   J 6 2   Declarer has two tricks. If East
    10 8 7 4   K 9 5   leads the suit, declarer ducks and
         A Q 3   can score three tricks.

(B2)   J 6 2   This is the same situation as (A2)
    Q 8 7 4   K 9 5   above. If East or West lead the
         A 10 3   suit, declarer can come to two
             tricks. If the defence never lead
             the suit, South has only one trick.

(B3)   J 6 2   Declarer has no trick and cannot
    A 10 8 4   K 9 5   come to a trick by leading this suit
         Q 7 3   from either hand. Yet if East or
             West lead the suit, South comes to
             a trick.

```
        K 9 6                    Declarer has two tricks only and will make
Q 7 5                10 8 4 3    only two by finessing the jack. This suit may
        A J 2                    seem innocuous to East, but if East starts
                                 the suit, declarer can score three tricks by
```
playing low from hand. The situation is similar to the above. East has an
honour and dummy holds the card below, the 9. That makes the switch
dangerous.

Do not mix up this situation with 'surround' plays. A surround position
exists when you sit over a high card and you have that card surrounded
(the one above and the one below) and you have a higher non-touching
honour as well. In that case, switching to the card above the surrounded
card is sound play. For example:

```
        J 6 4                    East is over dummy's jack and has the jack
8 5 2              A Q 10 7      surrounded (Q10) and a higher honour as
        K 9 3                    well. If East wants to lead this suit, the
                                 correct card is the queen, South covers and
```
the king wins. Now East has the A-10 over the jack and if West leads the
suit later, East takes the rest of the tricks in this suit and declarer makes
just one trick. If East leads a low card initially or switches to ace and
another, South can come to two tricks.

```
        9 5 2                    East is over dummy's 9 and has the 9
Q 4 3              K 10 8 7      surrounded, plus a higher honour as well.
        A J 6                    When switching to this suit, East should
                                 lead the 10. This holds declarer to one trick.
```
Leading the 7 allows South to duck to the 9 and score two tricks by
finessing the jack later.

```
        A 9 2                    East sits over dummy's 9 and has it
K 7 6              Q 10 8 5      surrounded and has a higher honour also. If
        J 4 3                    East decides to switch to this suit, East
                                 should lead the 10. This holds South to just
```
one trick. If East leads the 5, South can duck in hand, capture West's
king and score a second trick by leading to the jack later. If South started
with K-J-x, South always had three tricks by finessing the jack.

The memory aid for these positions (surround plus higher honour plus
sitting over the surround card) is to envisage the surrounded card in your
own hand. That would give you a sequence, so that you should lead top
of the imagined sequence.

TIP 43

Do not switch to a new suit if dummy has no long suit which can provide useful discards for declarer (and the bidding has not indicated declarer has a second long suit on which dummy's losers might be discarded).

(A)

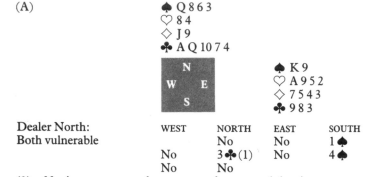

♠ Q 8 6 3
♡ 8 4
◇ J 9
♣ A Q 10 7 4

♠ K 9
♡ A 9 5 2
◇ 7 5 4 3
♣ 9 8 3

Dealer North:
Both vulnerable

WEST	NORTH	EAST	SOUTH
	No	No	1♠
No	3♣(1)	No	4♠
No	No		

(1)   Maximum pass, spade support and a strong club suit

West leads the queen of hearts and East wins with the ace, South playing the 3. How should East continue?

(B)

♠ Q 8 6 3 2
♡ 8 4
◇ A 9 2
♣ A 7 2

♠ K
♡ A 9 5 2
◇ 10 8 4 3
♣ 9 8 5 3

Dealer North:
Both vulnerable

WEST	NORTH	EAST	SOUTH
	No	No	1♠
No	3♠	No	4♠
No	No	No	

West leads the queen of hearts and East wins with the ace, South playing the 3. How should East continue?

Solutions: (A) South is marked with the ♡ K and you cannot score any more tricks in hearts. Dummy's clubs are menacing. If South has the ♣ K or ♣ J, South can take five club tricks and may discard losers in diamonds. It is vital to switch to a diamond at trick 2.

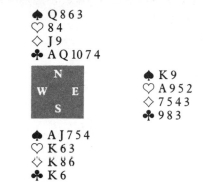

```
                        ♠ Q 8 6 3
                        ♡ 8 4
                        ◇ J 9
                        ♣ A Q 10 7 4
    ♠ 10 2                                   ♠ K 9
    ♡ Q J 10 7          N                    ♡ A 9 5 2
    ◇ A Q 10 2      W        E               ◇ 7 5 4 3
    ♣ J 5 2                                  ♣ 9 8 3
                        S
                        ♠ A J 7 5 4
                        ♡ K 6 3
                        ◇ K 8 6
                        ♣ K 6
```

You cannot defeat 4 ♠, but you can restrict the overtricks. If you return a heart, South can make 12 tricks. Win ♡ K, cross to ♣ Q, low spade to the jack, ♠ A, ♣ K, ruff a heart and discard three diamonds on the clubs. On the diamond return, South is limited to ten tricks and you have taken what's yours.

(B) Dummy has no long suit and South has shown no second suit. It is best here to go passive and not open a new suit. Return a heart.

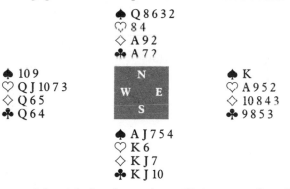

```
                        ♠ Q 8 6 3 2
                        ♡ 8 4
                        ◇ A 9 2
                        ♣ A 7 ?
    ♠ 10 9                                   ♠ K
    ♡ Q J 10 7 3        N                    ♡ A 9 5 2
    ◇ Q 6 5         W        E               ◇ 10 8 4 3
    ♣ Q 6 4                                  ♣ 9 8 5 3
                        S
                        ♠ A J 7 5 4
                        ♡ K 6
                        ◇ K J 7
                        ♣ K J 10
```

You cannot defeat 4 ♠, but the results are likely to range from 10 tricks to 12 tricks. Your job is to hold declarer to the minimum tricks. If you return a heart, declarer can score 11 tricks safely. Win ♡ K, diamond to the ace, trump, draw the last trump, cash ◇ K and exit with the ◇ J, endplaying the defence. However, some declarers will try for 12 tricks: win ♡ K, diamond to the ace, spade to the ace, spade to the queen, diamond to the jack. West can exit with a diamond and if declarer now plays East for the ♣ Q (split honours), declarer will make just 10 tricks.

However, if you switch to a club, you eliminate any club guess and declarer has 11 tricks. A diamond switch is even worse (*see* Tip 42 to see why). Declarer now has no diamond loser and if declarer picks the clubs correctly as well, declarer will score 12 tricks and a bottom for East-West.

TIP 44

In a cashout position, it is important to use count signals to enable partner to tell the number of tricks that can be cashed safely. The same applies to leads from 3-, 4- or 5-card suits in a cashout. The partnership should have a method which enables the number of cards in the leader's hand to be shown.

In giving count signals, you can use standard count (bottom from an odd number of cards and high-low with an even number) or reverse signals (bottom from an even number and high-low with an odd number). Reverse signals are slightly superior since you may not always be able to afford the top card from a doubleton. In a cashout situation, however, this is not likely to cost.

```
              ♠ A 8
              ♡ K J 7 3
              ◇ A Q 5
              ♣ Q J 6 4
                            ♠ 5 4
              N             ♡ A Q 8 4
          W       E         ◇ J 10 6
              S             ♣ A K 9 2
```

Dealer North:
Both vulnerable

WEST	NORTH	EAST	SOUTH
	1NT(1)	No	2♣
No	No	No	

(1)   15-17

West leads ♣ 8, 4 from dummy, king and South drops the 10. East is not fooled and cashes ♣ A, West following with the 3. East leads the ♣ 9 (high card for the higher suit back) and West ruffs. West switches to ♡ 2, king from dummy and South plays the 9 under East's ace. How should East continue?

Solution: It seems natural to play another club, partly to eliminate this winner and partly to give partner a chance to overruff dummy. However, there may be a better play at trick 5. Is there anything to guide you?

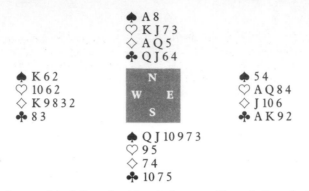

```
                    ♠ A 8
                    ♡ K J 7 3
                    ◇ A Q 5
                    ♣ Q J 6 4
  ♠ K 6 2              N              ♠ 5 4
  ♡ 10 6 2        W        E          ♡ A Q 8 4
  ◇ K 9 8 3 2                         ◇ J 10 6
  ♣ 8 3               S              ♣ A K 9 2
                    ♠ Q J 10 9 7 3
                    ♡ 9 5
                    ◇ 7 4
                    ♣ 10 7 5
```

On the actual deal, East should cash the second heart before playing
another club. This gives the defence six tricks and +100 will be some
compensation for East's failure to compete when 2 ♠ comes back to East.
(*See* TIP 17. East should double 2 ♠ and West will usually make 3 ◇ as
North has dreadful problems in defence.)

If East plays the fourth club before cashing the second heart, South will
discard the second heart. West will ruff but declarer can make the rest for
8 tricks and +110.

However, in standard methods West's ♡ 2 could be from 10-6-5-2 just as
well as 10-6-2. Declarer has done well to play as though he had a
singleton (rising with dummy's king and dropping the 9) and many an
East would be misled. If the ♡ 2 were from 10-6-5-2, it would be a
disaster to try to cash the second heart. South would ruff and could now
score 9 tricks. The spade finesse picks up West's king and after trumps
are drawn, South can discard any diamond losers on the ♡ J and the
♣ Q.

Whatever your normal methods for leads from 3-card or longer suits, it
pays you in a cashout situation to lead bottom card from a 3-card or
5-card suit (3rds and 5ths). The problem with leading the 2 from both
10-6-2 and 10-6-5-2 is that the length is difficult to diagnose when there is
only a one-card difference. When there is a two-card difference as with
3rds and 5ths, the situation is usually clearer. Partner can often tell that
the 5-card length is not possible.

3rds and 5ths may not clarify every problem, but will sort out the
position in cashouts much more often than 4th highest and bottom from
Honour-x-x. In the above case, West leads ♡ 2 and when the ace wins,
East knows West started with exactly three cards. Therefore, South has
another heart and East knows to cash the ♡ Q before playing the fourth
club.

TIP 45

There are many situations where you can gain an extra trick by declining to overruff declarer. This may be because the refusal to overruff promotes another trump in your hand or it may be because declarer misplaces the trump honours.

Situations such as these are quite well known:

	10 9 6 2	
A J		4
	K Q 8 7 5 3	

If East leads a suit where South and West are void, South may ruff with the K or Q. If West overruffs, West makes only one trick. If West discards, West scores two tricks.

	6 4 3	
K 7		J 10
	A Q 9 8 5 2	

If East leads a suit where South and West are void and South ruffs with the queen, West should overruff. West has no second trump that could become a winner if West discards. West's best chance, therefore, is to overruff and hope partner has a useful holding that could be promoted. If West overruffs, the defence has two trump tricks. If West discards, the defence takes only one trump trick. The same would apply if South had A Q J x x and East had 10-9-8.

	6 4	
Q 9 3 2		5
	A K J 10 8 7	

If East leads a suit where South and West are void, if South ruffs with the 8, West should overruff with the 9. If South ruffs with the jack, West should discard. An overruff with the queen would give West one trick only. South's remaining honours can draw all of West's trumps. Discarding allows West to come to two tricks. Do not overruff with an honour which will score a trick anyway, if there is a second card which could become promoted.

	J	
10 9		Q 7 5 3
	A K 8 6 4 2	

If East has a chance to overruff dummy, East should decline. The queen will win a trick anyway, and there are layouts where East can score a second trick by declining the overruff. If East does overruff, East makes one trick only.

```
          NORTH              Dealer East: Both vulnerable
          ♠ A Q 8 3          WEST    NORTH   EAST    SOUTH
          ♡ 5 3                              1♢      No
          ♢ Q 6 4            1♡      Dble    2NT(1)  No
          ♣ K Q J 10         4NT     No      5♡(2)   No
WEST                         6♡      No      No      6♠
♠ K 4 2        N             Dble    No      No      No
♡ A Q J 8 6 4  W    E
♢ A 7          S             (1)  Over the double, 2NT shows 6
♣ 6 2                        diamonds and 3 hearts and a good
                             opening.
                             (2)  Two key cards for hearts.
```

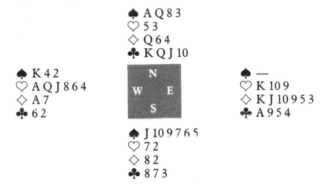

West leads ♢ A and another diamond, low from dummy and East wins
with the 9. East switches to ♡ 10 which wins, followed by ♡ K which
also wins. East then plays the ♢ K, ruffed by South with the jack of
spades. How should West play?

If South knew the location of the king of spades, it would be vital to take
the king of spades. Otherwise you may not make it. However, on the
bidding, the ♠ K could well be with East and, at the table, West did well
by discarding a club on the jack of spades without giving away any hint of
a problem.

This was the complete deal:

```
                    ♠ A Q 8 3
                    ♡ 5 3
                    ♢ Q 6 4
                    ♣ K Q J 10
        ♠ K 4 2          N          ♠ —
        ♡ A Q J 8 6 4  W    E       ♡ K 10 9
        ♢ A 7            S          ♢ K J 10 9 5 3
        ♣ 6 2                       ♣ A 9 5 4
                    ♠ J 10 9 7 6 5
                    ♡ 7 2
                    ♢ 8 2
                    ♣ 8 7 3
```

Declarer took the bait and led a spade to the ace, hoping to drop the
singleton ♠K with East. When West won the next spade, he led a club
to East's ace and ruffed the club return.

The bidding marked East with the ace of clubs. Had West overruffed the
jack of spades, the defence would take six tricks and score 1400, less than
the 1460 available in 6 ♡. Clearly not everyone would be sacrificing on
the South hand, so West felt that there would be little difference in
scoring +1400 or +1100. Both would outscore those in game and finish
behind those allowed to play in 6 ♡. It was, therefore, worth the risk of
scoring only 1100 in exchange for the chance of putting 6 ♠ doubled
seven down via the club ruff and obtaining an absolute top with +1700.

TIP 46

If dummy has a long running suit and no outside entry, you may be able to kill dummy's suit by leading that suit if either defender has more trumps than dummy (or the same number of trumps as dummy but your trumps are better than dummy's).

(A)

♠ J 7 3
♡ 10 8
♢ Q 4
♣ A Q J 8 7 3

♠ K 8 4
♡ K 4 2
♢ A K 8 7
♣ 10 5 2

	N	
W		E
	S	

Dealer South: Both vulnerable

WEST	NORTH	EAST	SOUTH
			1 ♡
No	2 ♣	No	3 ♡
No	4 ♡	All pass	

West leads the ace and king of diamonds, East following 2-6 and South 3-J. How should West continue at trick 3?

(B)

♠ 5 2
♡ 10 5 3
♢ A K Q J 6 5
♣ K 6

	N	
W		E
	S	

♠ Q 9
♡ 6
♢ 9
♣ A Q J 9 7 5 4 3 2

Dealer East: Nil vulnerable

WEST	NORTH	EAST	SOUTH
		5 ♣	5 ♠
No	6 ♢	No	6 ♠
No	No	No	

West leads the ♣ 8 and East wins, South following with the 10.

How should East continue?

Solutions: (A) West has 13 HCP and dummy has 10 HCP. In view of South's jump to 3 ♡, all the significant high cards missing should be with South. West will score the ♡ K but there is a strong chance that West will not come to a spade trick. East's diamond play has been discouraging and East will not have the queen of spades. South ought to hold ♠ A-Q on the bidding and if East had the ♠ Q, East could have played his highest diamond at trick 2, a secondary suit preference signal (*see* TIP 49) to show that whatever little East had was in spades.

As a diamond continuation cannot help and a spade switch is out, West should try a club switch. This proved a success on the actual deal as South held:

♠ A Q 10   ♡ A Q J 9 6 3   ♢ J 3   ♣ K 4

A second club after winning the ♡ K leaves declarer with no winning option.

(B) There are three reasonable choices after winning trick 1 and finding South with the remaining club. You could try a second club and hope to find West with the jack of spades. If so, the second club will promote a trump trick for the defence.

This is not likely to succeed. South has nothing in the minor suits and is missing the ♠ Q as well. It is highly likely that South's suit is headed by A-K-J. On the bidding, South is more likely to turn up with A-K-J-10-x-x-x than either A-K-10-x-x-x-x or A-K-10-x-x-x-x-x.

A second choice would be to switch to a heart and hope to find West with the ace of hearts. Again, with nothing in the minors and a spade suit missing the queen, it is improbable that South is missing the ace of hearts. South may have a heart loser but it is not likely to be the ace. An even more telling reason is that if West had the ♡ A, can you imagine West not leading it after this auction? Your 5-level opening may well have a singleton in hearts. How could West not try for a heart ruff if West had the ace?

The most promising switch is a diamond, hoping South has either a singleton diamond or a void. It will not hurt if South is void in diamonds since you can ruff the second diamond. It is not likely that one discard will be enough if South is missing the ♡ K or ♡ Q.

On the actual deal, the diamond switch was the winner:

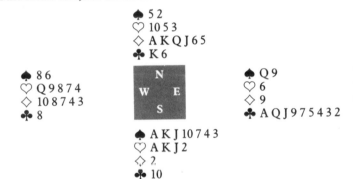

```
                    ♠ 5 2
                    ♡ 10 5 3
                    ◇ A K Q J 6 5
                    ♣ K 6
  ♠ 8 6                              ♠ Q 9
  ♡ Q 9 8 7 4         N              ♡ 6
  ◇ 10 8 7 4 3      W   E            ◇ 9
  ♣ 8                 S              ♣ A Q J 9 7 5 4 3 2
                    ♠ A K J 10 7 4 3
                    ♡ A K J 2
                    ◇ 2
                    ♣ 10
```

If you failed to find the diamond switch at trick 2, there is bad news and good news. The bad news is that South makes the slam. The good news is that you will have lots of company. When this deal arose, 6♠ was allowed to make at many tables. It is true that North could have found the winning bid of 6NT which is unbeatable played by North. That is none of your concern and it will enter the conversation only if you managed to defeat 6♠.

TIP 47

When partner leads from an interior sequence or from a broken sequence, be quick to drop an honour if you can afford it so that the position will be clarified for partner.

We all understand Murphy's First Law of Defence: 'If you give partner a chance to go wrong, partner will take that chance.'

There are many occasions when partner will lead from an honour combination and will be unable to tell whether you or declarer has the missing honour. If you can clear up the position for partner without loss, do so. In addition, partner will expect such help and if it is not forthcoming, partner will place the missing honour with declarer. You will have no answer to the charge of being declarer's accomplice if you fail to drop your honour card.

	K 9	
A J 10 8 4		Q 5 3
	7 6 2	

In no-trumps, West leads the jack and declarer plays the king from dummy. Which card should East play?

West's lead of the jack could be from an interior sequence or from a sequence headed by J-10-8. In either case it cannot hurt East to drop the queen. On the actual layout, West's suit is set up and West knows it. If East had played an encouraging 5, West might read the position to be:

	K 9	
A J 10 8 4		7 6 5
	Q 3 2	

If so, West on gaining the lead might shift to some other suit, aiming to find East's entry so that East can lead through declarer's holding.

If West's suit were J-10-8-x-x, East's queen will enable West to set up the suit with one more lead. If East withholds the queen, West may decide there is no future in the suit and shift to something else.

♠ A Q J 6
♡ A 4
♢ J 10 9
♣ J 6 4 3

Dealer South: Nil vulnerable

WEST	NORTH	EAST	SOUTH
			1NT(1)
No	3NT	All pass	
(1)	15-17		

N
W E
S

♠ 9 5
♡ K 10 6
♢ 8 3 2
♣ K 10 7 5 2

West leads the queen of hearts and declarer plays the ace from dummy. Which card should East play?

At the table, East followed with 6 of hearts (East-West were using reverse signals so low was encouraging), but that was no success. This was the complete deal:

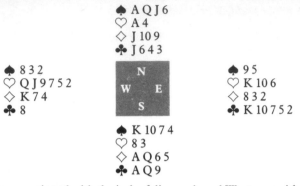

```
                    ♠ A Q J 6
                    ♡ A 4
                    ♢ J 10 9
                    ♣ J 6 4 3
    ♠ 8 3 2                        ♠ 9 5
    ♡ Q J 9 7 5 2     N            ♡ K 10 6
    ♢ K 7 4       W       E        ♢ 8 3 2
    ♣ 8               S            ♣ K 10 7 5 2
                    ♠ K 10 7 4
                    ♡ 8 3
                    ♢ A Q 6 5
                    ♣ A Q 9
```

Declarer continued with the jack of diamonds and West won with the king. West switched to a spade and not only was the contract not defeated, but East-West scored a near-bottom as South's 3NT outscored most of those in 4 ♠.

East ought to have played the 10 of hearts to clarify the position for West. East knows that West has led from a Q-J-9 sequence, but West does not know East's holding. The 10 will solidify West's holding, so that West will know it is safe to play a second heart no matter where the king is.

Dropping the 6 as a come-on signal may be clear to East, but West might well read it as a singleton. That would give South K-10-8-3, certainly a possibility, and now a second round of hearts would give declarer a present of a third heart trick.

Dropping the king is better than the 6, but that is also risky. Again this might be a singleton, giving South 10-8-6-3 and if West cashes the jack of hearts when in with the ♢ K, it would give South an extra trick in hearts which South could not develop himself.

The ♡ 10 allows West to continue the hearts without risk. Then East can overtake with the king and return the 6. That will teach North to use Stayman next time.

TIP 48

When your play within a suit is immaterial to you and cannot assist partner in regard to that suit, the card you play can be utilised as a suit preference signal.

```
        643
KQJ82        95
        A 10 7
```

Against no-trumps West leads the king and South holds off. West leads the queen and again South lets it go. West has J-8-2 left and knows that the next lead will knock out the ace. It is immaterial to West whether the J, 8 or 2 is led and it makes no difference to East either as far as the suit itself is concerned. West therefore uses the opportunity to signal the outside entry, the information which is useful to East: lead the jack, high card for high suit entry; lead the 2, lowest card, for low suit entry; lead the 8, middle card, for middle suit entry.

(A)

```
♠ K 2
♡ J 10 8
♢ A K J 9
♣ A Q J 10
```

Dealer East: Nil vulnerable

WEST	NORTH	EAST	SOUTH
		1♡	2♠(1)
No	4♠	All pass	

(1) Weak

```
     N
  W     E
     S
```

```
♠ 764
♡ A K Q 5 3
♢ —
♣ K 8 6 5 2
```

West leads the ♡9. How should East plan the defence?

Be specific about the actual order in which East should play the hearts chosen.

(B)

```
♠ K Q J 4
♡ K Q J 8
♢ J 8 3
♣ 5 3
```

Dealer East: Nil vulnerable

WEST	NORTH	EAST	SOUTH
		3♣	No
No	Dble	No	4♡
No	No	No	

```
     N
  W     E
     S
```

```
♠ 10 2
♡ 10
♢ K 7 2
♣ K J 10 9 8 4 2
```

West leads the 7 of clubs. How should East plan the defence?

Solutions: (A) West's 9 lead is clearly a singleton or top of a doubleton. East desperately wants a diamond ruff. East can achieve that by cashing two hearts and forcing West to ruff the third heart. (Cashing the top three hearts will not work as West is then unlikely to ruff the third heart.) When giving West the ruff, East will lead the 5 of hearts, the higher remaining card as a suit preference for diamonds. A good defender will know that the 5 is the higher heart, but many Wests will not be sure. They will have forgotten to take note of the spot cards on the first two tricks.

East can improve the chances of West finding the diamond shift. Win trick one with the ace of hearts and trick two with the king of hearts. This abnormal order of winning in third seat is used as a suit-preference signal for the higher suit outside trumps. Thus the order is ♡A, ♡K then ♡5 and hope West is on the same wavelength.

(B)   What do you make of the ♣ 7 lead? It is either a singlton or the top from 7-6 doubleton. South therefore has A-Q-6 or A-Q and it is irrelevant to you which card you play. South will make two tricks regardless. However, if partner's lead is a singleton, partner needs to know your outside entry. The only possible entry is via the king of diamonds. East should therefore follow to trick one with the 2 of clubs: lowest card = low suit entry. Unfortunately this would not occur to a number of players who would follow mechanically third-hand-high. They thus miss a golden opportunity to furnish partner with highly useful information.

The complete deal:

♠ K Q J 4
♡ K Q J 8
♢ J 8 3
♣ 5 3

<table>
<tr>
<td>
♠ 9 8 7 3
♡ A 4
♢ A 10 9 6 5 4
♣ 7
</td>
<td></td>
<td>
♠ 10 2
♡ 10
♢ K 7 2
♣ K J 10 9 8 4 2
</td>
</tr>
</table>

♠ A 6 5
♡ 9 7 6 5 3 2
♢ Q
♣ A Q 6

At the table, East did follow with the 2 of clubs at trick 1 and West understood the message. West won the heart lead at trick 2 and switched to the 9 of diamonds. East won with the king and read the ♢9 switch correctly as not wanting a diamond back. East returned a club ruffed by West. West tried to cash the ♢A, but South ruffed and had the rest.

South made 4♡ for +420, but this neat defence was worth a near-top to East-West. There were plenty of 450s for North-South on the scoresheet.

Note that if West had started with 7-6 in clubs, then the shift to diamonds should be ♢A and another diamond. Also, if East held something like ♠ — ♡xxx ♢Qxx ♣K J 10 9 8 4 2 or perhaps even ♠Ax ♡x ♢xxx ♣K J 10 9 8 4 2, East should play the king of clubs or preferably the jack of clubs, a high card asking for the high suit if West happens to come in with the ♡A.

TIP 49

You can help partner find the best shift by the use of secondary suit preference signals.

A primary signal is the signal given by the first card you play in the given suit, whether it is an attitude signal or a count signal. After that primary message has been sent, you may have more than one card left in that suit. If so, the next card chosen (the second card or the secondary signal) can be used for a suit preference message.

For example, suppose you play the 2 first from 9-5-2 as a discouraging signal. On the next round you can play the 9 as a preference for the high suit and the 5 as no preference for the high suit. Or, suppose you play the 8 first from 8-7-6-3 to show an even number of cards. On the next round, you can play the 7 as a preference for the high suit and the 3 as no preference for the high suit.

(A)

♠ A Q 8 3
♡ 8 6 5 2
◇ 7 4
♣ A J 9

♠ 10 5
♡ K J 9 4 3
◇ Q 8 2
♣ 7 6 4

Dealer South: Nil vulnerable

WEST	NORTH	EAST	SOUTH
			1♣
2◇(1)	Dble	3◇	3♠
No		4♠	All pass

(1) Weak

West cashes ◇ A and East plays ◇ 2, discouraging. West continues with ◇ K. How should East defend?

(B)

♠ A 9 6 3
♡ Q 4
◇ 10 9 5 4
♣ K 7 2

♠ 2
♡ 5 3
◇ K Q J 7
♣ J 9 8 6 4 3

Dealer East: Both vulnerable

WEST	NORTH	EAST	SOUTH
		No	1♣(1)
No	1NT	No	2♣(2)
No	2♡(3)	No	3♠(4)
No	4♣(5)	No	4NT
No	5◇	No	6♠
No	No	No	

(1) Precision   (2) Stayman-like
(3) Minimum with spades
(4) Sets spades as trumps
(5) No ace outside trumps

West leads the 2 of diamonds (3rds/5ths) and East's jack is taken by the ace. South cashes the ♠ K : 4-3-2, followed by the ♠ Q : 5-6-club discard. South continues with the ◇ 8 : 3-5 and East wins with the queen. How should East continue?

(A) On the second diamond East should follow with the queen. This is intended as a suit-preference message for hearts. There is some risk that West may take you for queen-doubleton in diamonds, but the risk is small and is worth taking. Firstly, you supported diamonds and so figure to have three diamonds rather than two. Secondly, South's play may clarify the position. On the actual deal South had J-3 and with J-8-3, South would not drop the jack on the second round as the jack is now high. Thirdly, dummy's trumps are so strong that it is not likely that East is trying for an overruff or a promotion position.

Anyway, such risks have to be taken occasionally to try to steer partner to the right shift. Looking at dummy, East would expect West to be more likely to switch to clubs than hearts.

For the aftermath of this deal, *see* TIP 14.

(B) East must find the right shift at this moment. What are the clues? West has shown three diamonds. West led the 2 and next followed with the 3. The lowest remaining diamond implies interest for the lower suit outside trumps (or at least no interest for the higher outside suit). East should return a club.

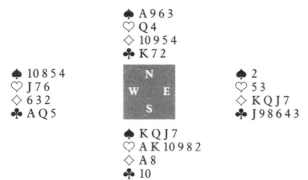

```
                    ♠ A 9 6 3
                    ♡ Q 4
                    ◇ 10 9 5 4
                    ♣ K 7 2
    ♠ 10 8 5 4          N           ♠ 2
    ♡ J 7 6                          ♡ 5 3
    ◇ 6 3 2        W        E        ◇ K Q J 7
    ♣ A Q 5            S             ♣ J 9 8 6 4 3
                    ♠ K Q J 7
                    ♡ A K 10 9 8 2
                    ◇ A 8
                    ♣ 10
```

West hit on the diamond lead, the only lead to shoot the slam. When declarer found the snag with the bad trump break, declarer led a diamond, hoping that the winner would not hold the ♣ A. Declarer's plan was to win say a heart return with the queen, ruff a diamond high, finesse the 9 of spades and come home on the hearts after drawing the last trump.

In addition to the secondary signal in diamonds, West has given a secondary signal in trumps. The ♠ 4 showed an even number of spades and the ♠ 5 next, the lowest remaining spade, was also intended to show preference for the low suit rather than the high suit. When you can afford it you can utilise such secondary suit preference messages in the trump suit, too.

126

TIP 50

When it comes down to the last two cards, it is vital for you to know which card to keep and which to let go. Beware of becoming a victim of the 'Memory Coup'. When partner discards a winner late in the play, it means partner has only winners left. It is safe therefore to lead to partner and let partner cash the rest of the tricks.

There are lots of clues available about what to hold and what to pitch at trick 12 or thereabouts. If declarer could ruff a suit in dummy but has not done so, declarer has no more cards in that suit. Note when declarer shows out of a suit so that you know later you can discard that suit if declarer is still in hand at trick 11 or 12.

If partner has shown out of a suit, you can work out the number of cards with which declarer started. Keep track of those cards so that you will know whether declarer has any cards of that suit left at the end.

Count signals are also helpful. If partner's signal indicates the number of cards partner holds, you can deduce the number of cards with which declarer started. Again, a careful watch will help you know what is left at the end. It is rarely a genuine guess what to keep and what to let go.

Secondary count signals may also be used later in the play. When it is clear that high cards are no longer relevant and that the problem is what to keep, players use 'present count signals'. With an even number of cards remaining, follow or discard high-then-low. With an odd number left, follow or discard from the bottom up. If partner is watching, partner can work out the number of cards you have left in the suit and hence the number of cards declarer has.

The problem, of course, is that some defenders do not keep such a careful watch. When declarer tables the last card, a defender may gasp with dismay at finding that the wrong card was kept and declarer has stolen a trick. Then come the silent vows about 'I promise to watch the cards in future, I promise, I promise . . .'

♠ K Q 8 5 4
♡ A 9 8 7
◇ 8
♣ 10 6 5

Dealer East: Nil vulnerable

WEST	NORTH	EAST	SOUTH
		No	1◇
No	1♠	No	2◇
No	2♡	No	2NT
No	No	No	

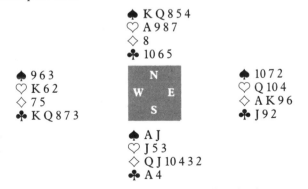

♠ 10 7 2
♡ Q 10 4
◇ A K 9 6
♣ J 9 2

1. West leads the 7 of clubs (fourth highest): 5-9-4.
2. East continues with the jack of clubs: ace-3-6.
3–4: South cashes ♠ A and ♠ J, West follows: 3-6.
5. South leads the ♡ 5 to the ace, West following with the 2.
6–8: Dummy's spades are cashed. South throws ◇ 2, ◇ 3, ◇ 4. West follows once, then discards the ◇ 5 and ♡ 6. East discards 9-6 in diamonds.
9. Declarer leads the ♡ 9 from dummy: 10-5-K.
10. West cashes the ♣ K, South discards the ♡ J.
11. West cashes the ♣ Q and East is down to ♡ Q, ◇ A-K. which card should East discard? South discards the jack of diamonds.
12. West cashes the ♣ 8. Which card should East keep?

Aaagghh! Exactly the problem you want to avoid. If you have been keeping a close track of the cards as they fall, you will know that you should hold the . . . winner in diamonds. If you did keep the diamond, well done as West's last card is the ◇ 7.

However, the problem should never have arisen. At trick 11, East should discard the ace of diamonds. This indicates that East has nothing but winners left and asks partner to lead a diamond or a heart so that East will not have the terrible guess at trick 12. West should therefore not cash the fifth club but should lead the diamond at trick 12. Spare partner the guess and partner will not guess wrong.

The complete deal:

```
                 ♠ K Q 8 5 4
                 ♡ A 9 8 7
                 ◇ 8
                 ♣ 10 6 5
  ♠ 9 6 3                          ♠ 10 7 2
  ♡ K 6 2          N               ♡ Q 10 4
  ◇ 7 5        W       E           ◇ A K 9 6
  ♣ K Q 8 7 3      S               ♣ J 9 2
                 ♠ A J
                 ♡ J 5 3
                 ◇ Q J 10 4 3 2
                 ♣ A 4
```

2♠ would have been easier for North-South, but that is not your concern as defender. Your job is not to let them get away with 120.